THE BLOOMER GIRLS

Amelia Bloomer in 1851. Daguerreotype by T. W. Brown.

CHARLES NEILSON GATTEY

THE
BLOOMER
GIRLS

FOREWORD BY JAMES LAVER

Coward-McCann, Inc. New York

TO MY MOTHER

COPYRIGHT © 1967 BY CHARLES NEILSON GATTEY

FIRST AMERICAN EDITION 1968

Library of Congress Catalog Card Number: 68-23366

PRINTED IN THE UNITED STATES OF AMERICA

ACKNOWLEDGEMENTS

For permission to examine old records and to obtain photographs and for assistance in my researches, my thanks are due to the New York Public Library; Miss Mildred K. Smock, Librarian of the Council Bluffs Public Library; Mrs. Shirley Patterson, Director of the Seneca Falls Historical Society's Museum; Mrs. Woodrow M. Donovan, Curator of Manuscripts at the Schlesinger Library, Radcliffe College, Cambridge, Massachusetts; the British Museum; the Victoria and Albert Museum; the Radio Times Hulton Picture Library; Raymond Mander and Joe Mitchenson; and also to all those kind people who have made available to me so far unpublished letters and diaries of the period.

C. N. G.

CONTENTS

LIST OF ILLUSTRATIONS

First HOME of Mr. and Mrs. DEXTER C. BLOOMER—Seneca Falls, N.Y.

FOREWORD

by James Laver, c.b.e.

R EFORMERS' HAVE arisen in all ages but until the middle of the nineteenth century most of them were men. A solitary figure like Mary Wollstonecraft merely confirmed the general opinion that feminine revolt was just another name for atheism and free love. Fifty years later, however, the climate had changed. The demand for women's rights began to be linked with all kinds of crusades for the betterment of mankind, and these crusades were promoted with evangelical fervour. The embattled ladies now had no doubt that God was on their side, and they managed to persuade a number of men to the same opinion.

It is no accident that the majority of the ladies in question were to be found in the United States of America, or at least in the northern half of the Republic. It was partly a matter of the pioneering tradition. The women who had trekked across a continent with their menfolk, who had helped to fight off the Indians, who had tilled the virgin land and established a homestead in the wilderness, could not be dismissed as playthings whose only function in life was sex and the solace of the male. Yet the law still treated them as half-witted children, unfit to make decisions or have control of any property of their own.

The first enemy to be attacked was drink, and in this almost all women were on the side of the reformers. A witty Frenchman put it very neatly when remarking "Venus has never forgiven Bacchus for dividing with her the allegiance of mankind".

The prudist wing of the reforming army also objected very strongly to nudity, even in painting and classical statues in public galleries, and even more strongly to any display of the female body on the stage. They insisted that women should be wrapped up from head to foot in garments which gave no hint of the underlying anatomy; and it was here, of course, that they parted company with the body of reformers led by Mrs. Bloomer.

Amelia Bloomer was no fanatic (except perhaps in the matter of temperance) and she saw clearly that women would never be able to attain their freedom if they continued to wear the hampering garments which were the very symbol of their servitude. Her protest, naturally enough, took a tough moral line, as when she begged the "Daughters of the American Republic" to "abjure the feminine fashion adopted at profligate courts in Europe".

That was to strike the right note but, unfortunately, the dress proposed by Mrs. Bloomer seemed to many of her contemporaries to be itself, if not profligate, at least unfeminine and improper. To us, today, this seems a very strange judgment. The skirt reached to half-way between the knee and the ankle—and as recently as the eighteen-thirties it had not been very much longer than this. Nor were the legs exposed, for under the skirt there were trousers "cut moderately full and gathered in above the footwear".

This sounds—and looked—feminine enough, but it was the trousers that caused all the excitement. For the mid-Victorians in England and their American contemporaries certainly had a complex about trousers. They shied away from the very word and, failing to find any other to replace it, were reduced to referring to them as 'inexpressibles'. Trousers were the symbol of the male and of male domination and the proposal that women should adopt them (almost entirely concealed by the skirt as they were) was seen as a threat to the whole structure of society.

In the long perspective of costume history this is, of course, nonsense. There is nothing *inevitably* masculine about bifurcated garments or *inevitably* feminine about skirts. The Roman legions were as much kilted (i.e. skirted) as the Scottish highlanders. Turkish and Chinese women wore trousers. The anthropologists distinguish not between male and female garments but between 'arctic' and 'tropical' dress. But for some hundreds of years in Western Europe trousers had been the prerogative of men and for a woman to 'wear the trousers', even in a metaphorical sense, seemed to imply the reversal of all established values. One can only wonder what those who objected to the Bloomer Costume and even Mrs. Bloomer herself would have thought of the dress of young people today when it is often difficult to decide which is the boy and which the girl.

Much has been written about Bloomers but little about Mrs. Bloomer, the woman herself, until now. The present work concerns not only her but also all those who rallied round her and fought her battles—the

Bloomer Girls. Mr. Neilson Gattey has certainly explored his sources to some purpose and has produced a real contribution to social history. Mrs. Bloomer has indeed had her revenge and we should be grateful to this singular woman who gave the world so useful a plural.

JAMES LAVER.

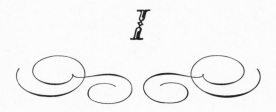

THE WATER BUCKET

THREE WOMEN became brides in the year 1840 who were destined to influence the world in which they lived in contrasting ways.

Queen Victoria married Prince Albert, whilst in America Elizabeth Cady wed Henry Stanton and Amelia Jenks became Mrs. Dexter C. Bloomer. These last two weddings had one unusual feature in common; the word "obey" was deliberately omitted from the women's vows.

Elizabeth Cady Stanton, the American forerunner of Mrs. Pankhurst, enters our story later. Our present concern is with Amelia, the blue-eyed, auburn-haired little woman with the winning smile, who was to startle her contemporaries by appearing in a daring new form of dress, not only in the main thoroughfares of crowded cities, but also in the full limelight of the lecture platform. No one who knew her in the early days could have foretold such a future for her.

The woman whose name is in every English dictionary was born on May 27th, 1818, in the town of Homer in the State of New York. She was the youngest child of Ananias Jenks, a man of forceful character, clothier by trade, and his wife Lucy, a devoutly religious woman. Amelia had the limited education of a girl of those days and, when she was seventeen, taught for a brief period in a school until her family moved to Waterloo in the same State. There, in 1837, she became governess to the three youngest children of a Mr. and Mrs. Chamberlain.

Amelia was very popular with her pupils and also made many friends in the district. The most important of these to her was a young man who lived in the nearby small town of Seneca Falls, where he studied law. He was extremely interested in politics, being editor and part owner of the local Whig paper, the *Seneca County Courier*. Their friendship soon turned to love and they were married on April 15th, 1840, in the house of a friend, by the Rev. Samuel H. Gridley, a Presbyterian clergyman.

The bridegroom was aged twenty-four, a Quaker, tall and slim, with grey eyes and a high forehead, and —to quote his own words—of "a bashful and reserved demeanour". With a lawyer's concern for detail, he also recorded that he weighed a hundred and fifty pounds at the time, and Amelia only one hundred, which he considered right for her height—five foot four inches.

The day after their marriage, the young couple drove in a carriage to the home in Seneca Falls of Mr. Isaac Fuller, Dexter's partner in the printing business, who had rented them part of his house. That evening a party was held in their honour, and the rooms were merry with the chatter of well-wishers, who had arrived accompanied by a band. Refreshments included wine and all, or nearly all, partook of it. But when Dexter

16

offered a glass to Amelia, she refused. "What—will you not drink a glass of wine with me on this joyful occasion?" he asked. "Surely it can do you no harm?" But his wife shook her head. "No, I cannot—I must not," she smiled.

It is the fashion nowadays to mock the Victorians' horror-hate of the Demon Drink. But everyone who has studied closely the social conditions of the period will find strong support for their attitude. Drunkenness was a very real evil in mid-nineteenth-century America. Cheap rum poured into the country from the West Indies, farms made their own whisky, and in the towns few workmen would take a job unless they received, as an addition to their wages, a plentiful supply of hard liquor.

As a reaction to this state of affairs, in the year of Amelia's marriage, there swept over the country a movement known as the Great Washingtonian Temperance Reformation, led by the Seven Reformed Drunkards of Baltimore. These men met in a saloon in that city and, sobered by the death of one of their friends, resolved that they would drink no more and that they would devote the rest of their lives to touring the country, advocating total abstinence. One of the Seven became a backslider, but the other Six lived and died, honouring the cause they had embraced.

Pollard and Wright, two of the Reformed Men, visited Seneca Falls and held meetings there. They stayed with the Bloomers and, as a result, Amelia helped to found the local Temperance Society, and became a regular contributor to its mouthpiece, *The Water Bucket*.

An extract from an article written in 1842 by Mrs. Bloomer shows her hitting back at those ladies who claimed that some alcohol was indispensable to good cooking.

"Brandy in apple dumplings, forsooth! That lady must be a wretched cook indeed who cannot make a dumpling, mince pies, or cake, palatable without the addition of poisonous substances. But I would ask these ladies if they had ever tried to do without it? Their answer, I fear, would be in the negative. They do not wish to do without it.

"What examples these ladies are setting before their families! Have they a husband, a son or a brother, and have they no fear that the examples they are now setting them may be the means of their filling a drunkard's grave? . . ."

Mrs. Bloomer signed this article with her favourite pseudonym, "Gloriana". In another piece, she informed her readers that ninety thousand houses were licensed by the British Government for the sale of intoxicating liquor, and that the people of that small island spent $400,000,000 per annum on the stuff.

With disapproval and regret, she commented on the fact that there were "over four thousand princes in Germany who received from the people over $200,000,000, whilst a labourer worked eighteen hours out of twenty-four for 72 cents per week".

Amelia's efforts on behalf of temperance must have been very successful, for soon she was able to record with pride the enrolment of the five hundredth member of the Society.

This Temperance work gave Mrs. Bloomer much satisfaction. She felt she was doing something supremely worth-while in guarding the moral and physical health of the delightful little town in which she lived. She loved its wide, tree-lined streets and its wonderful, bracing air. The house into which she had moved in

18

October, 1840, was a modest one, but she did not mind, for there was such a wealth of natural beauty around her.

Seneca Falls lies on a river at the head of the largest of the Finger Lakes. In 1827, the population had been only two hundred and sixty-five, but in 1840 it had risen to three thousand five hundred, and there were nearly five hundred dwellings. Already there were many mills taking advantage of its plentiful water power; seven for flour, four for plaster, two for oil, and six sawing timber. There were also three sash and window-blind factories, a clock factory, a clothing factory, and twenty stores. On the debit side, from Mrs. Bloomer's point of view, was the town's solitary distillery and its four taverns.

"Seneca Lake is the most beautiful of the numerous lakes which adorn western New York," states the *Gazeteer of the State of New York* for 1842. "It extends from south to west forty miles, and varies in width from two to four miles. It is very deep, and in consequence is never frozen. The water is very clear. The lands about the southern extremity of the lake are high and picturesque; about the northern less elevated, but undulating and covered with the richest crops, with here and there remains of the magnificent primitive forest."

In this little paradise, Amelia might have happily spent the rest of her life attending Temperance gatherings, and writing for *The Water Bucket,* had not Mrs. Elizabeth Cady Stanton come to live there in 1847.

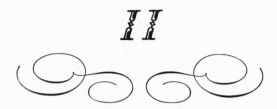

THE FIRST WOMEN'S RIGHTS
CONVENTION

ELIZABETH CADY STANTON was three years older
than Amelia. She was born on November 12th,
1815, the very day her father, Judge Daniel Cady,
was elected to Congress. When she was a child, many
an unfortunate woman would call and beg for the
Judge's help. She would listen with growing pity to
what they had to say. Men were often cruel to their
wives, she learned, and the law supported them. Surely
it was unjust for a man to make his wife give him her
earnings and squander them when their children lacked
bread? Surely it was illegal for him to beat her, to lock
her in a room, and to deprive her of all intercourse with
her friends? Surely he had no right to take her children
and prevent her from ever seeing them again? But
Daniel Cady could do nothing for them. And when
they refused to believe him, he would open his law books
and read aloud to them the sections of the statutes
relevant to the case. There was no hope for them—
none.

After they had left, Elizabeth would pore over these harsh laws and promise herself that one day she would do something to right such wrongs.

She read in Professor Walker's *Introduction to American Law*: "The legal theory is, marriage makes the husband and wife one person, and that person is the husband. There is scarcely a legal act of any description that she is competent to perform ... In Ohio, but hardly anywhere else, is she allowed to make a will, if happily she has anything to dispose of."

In Roper's *Law of Husband and Wife,* she learned: "It is not generally known, that whenever a woman has accepted an offer of marriage, all she has, or expects to have, becomes virtually the property of the man thus accepted as a husband; and no gift or deed executed by her between the period of acceptance and the marriage is held to be valid; for were she permitted to give away or otherwise settle her property, he might be disappointed in the wealth he looked to in making the offer."

"The wife is only the servant of her husband", proclaimed *Wharton's Laws*.

Elizabeth was horrified to discover that wife beating was sanctioned by law.

Judge Cady had only one son who died at the age of eleven and in his great grief, Elizabeth's father said: "Oh, my daughter, would that you were a boy!"

Roused by these words, the girl made up her mind to become as proficient as a man in as many pursuits as possible. At Johnstown Academy, she was the only one of her sex in the classes for Latin, Greek and Higher Mathematics, as well as the best horseback rider.

She was an impressionable girl and later, when in her teens, an incident took place which influenced her outlook for the rest of her life. She was the leader of the Presbyterian Girls' Club in her home town. One of its aims was to collect funds to pay for the training of a promising candidate for the Ministry. The girls spent months sewing clothes and selling them, baking cakes and making sweets and jams and holding fairs to dispose of them. They organized concerts and other entertainments and, after a long struggle and much hard work, they raised enough money to pay the fees of a selected student at Auburn Theological Seminary. When he had taken his degree, they collected together amongst themselves a sum of money sufficient to buy him a new suit of black broadcloth, and asked him to address them in their church.

The occasion received a great deal of publicity and the church was packed. The members of the Girls' Club, dressed in their best, sat proudly in the front pews, admiring the young Minister in the suit which he had purchased with the money they had sent him. When he rose to preach his sermon, they modestly looked away, expecting him to begin by thanking them for all they had done. But, instead, he announced as his text this verse from Timothy, "But I suffer not a woman to teach, nor to usurp authority over the man, but to be in silence."

The girls stared at one another in amazement. A look of contempt came over Elizabeth's face and, signalling to her companions to follow her, she led them out of the church. Never again did she help in any way towards the training of young men as ministers.

When she was twenty-four, Elizabeth fell in love with a handsome, eloquent young Abolitionist, Henry B. Stanton, and married him on May 10th, 1840. They decided to spend their honeymoon touring Europe and attending the World's Anti-Slavery Convention in London. In America, women had played a prominent part working for the movement and, as the invitations sent out from London had made no qualifying reference to sex, several women supporters travelled over as well. Many of them were Quakers. Most prominent among the latter was Mrs. Lucretia Mott, a charming, cultured humanitarian, some twenty-two years older than young Mrs. Stanton. The two women took to one another and became close friends.

The news of the impending arrival of the women delegates was first broken to the organizers by some American clergymen, whose ship reached England in advance of the main party. The nine women concerned were portrayed as being formidable and belligerent Amazons, and the anxious officials conferred together on the problem of how to prevent them from attending the Convention, when it opened on Friday, June 12th, in the Freemasons' Hall, Great Queen Street, in Lincoln's Inn Fields.

The committee found it hard to concentrate on the matter for, in the middle of their deliberations, there came disquieting news. At about six o'clock in the evening of Wednesday, June 10th, Queen Victoria and Prince Albert had left Buckingham Palace by the Garden Gate in a very low German droshky. A number of respectable people had assembled outside to witness her departure and were ranged in two lines. After the carriage had proceeded some distance up Constitution Hill, a young man who was standing with his back to the railings, pulled out a pistol and fired it at Her Majesty, there being no one between him and the carriage.

The Prince, it seemed, heard the whistling of the ball and turned his head in the direction from which the report came. The Queen at the same instant rose up in the carriage, but Prince Albert pulled her down by his side.

The man then shouted, "I have another!" and drawing a second pistol from behind his back, discharged it after the carriage, which had by that time passed him a little.

The Times next day reported that the perpetrator of this outrage was immediately seized, and that neither Her Majesty or Prince Albert evinced any indication of alarm or excitement at the deadly attack from which they had so providentially escaped. "The name of the ruffian is Edward Oxford and he is said to be a person out of place."

Feeling that after such an outrage, it would not do for the Convention's image to be tarnished by the participation of such apparently revolutionary radicals as the American females were reported to be, Mr. Tredgold, the secretary of the British and Foreign Anti-Slavery Society, himself called on the unwelcome visitors at their hotel. He was extremely relieved to find them to be "women of refinement". Nevertheless, he appealed to them to stay away and not to risk causing discord.

Having travelled all the way from America, the nine ladies were naturally extremely annoyed and, insisting on their rights, attended the opening session in the company of Lady Byron and Miss Elizabeth Fry.

Before anyone could challenge the right of the women to be present, the head of the American delegation, Wendell Phillips, proposed that a Committee of Five be appointed to prepare a correct list of the members of the Convention, with instructions to include all persons bearing credentials from any Anti-Slavery body. There were immediate shouts of "Turn out the women!" from the American clergymen.

Dr. Bowring, an English delegate, rose to support Wendell Phillips' resolution. "In this country," he pointed out, "sovereign rule is placed in the hands of a female, and one who has been exercising her influence in opposing slavery by sanctioning the presence of her illustrious Consort at an Anti-Slavery meeting. We are associated with a body of Christians (Quakers) who have given their women great prominence. I look upon this delegation from America as one of the most interesting and encouraging symptoms of the times. I cannot believe that we shall refuse to welcome gratefully the co-operation of these ladies."

The debate that followed was a heated one, but the women themselves remained silent, calm, and dignified throughout. An English clergyman, the Rev. J. Burnet, declared that it would be better for the Convention to be dissolved at once, rather than allow women to take part. The Rev. Henry Grew, an American from Philadelphia, agreed, saying that the presence of females would be "a violation of the ordinances of Almighty God". Captain Wanchope, R.N., delegate from Carlisle, entreated the ladies not to push the question too far, but to gracefully retire, lest Anglo-American relations be harmed.

At last, the vote was taken, and the women were excluded by the overwhelming majority of the delegates. As they were already in the hall, they were asked to sit in a recess behind a bar and a curtain, similar to those in churches to screen the choir from the public gaze.

The great American Abolitionist, William Lloyd Garrison, having been delayed at sea, arrived too late to take part in the debate. When he heard that the women had been rejected as delegates, he refused to take his seat on the platform and retired to the public gallery where he remained a silent spectator of the proceedings which lasted ten days.

Although the women had lost the battle that day, they had gained much publicity and had focused the attention of the world on the parlous state of their sex, making all liberally disposed people feel that it was time something were done to improve it.

As Lucretia Mott and Elizabeth Cady Stanton walked arm-in-arm down Great Queen Street that night, discussing the stormy session, they made up their minds, first, to hold a Women's Rights Convention on their return to America and, second, that the first slaves to be freed in the world were the white women of their own country. Walking down Great Queen Street today, Lucretia and Elizabeth might be surprised to learn the rate of progress made by the anti-slavery movement over a hundred and twenty years later. In February, 1967, it was reported to the United Nations' Commission on Human Rights, meeting in Geneva, that there were still just over two million slaves in the modern world, most of these women in Africa and Asia.

Meanwhile the ladies made up for not being allowed to speak in the Freemasons' Hall by keeping up a brisk fire at their hotel on the American clergymen who were staying there. Some promptly moved with their luggage to another hotel, but the Rev. Nathaniel Colver from Boston, who always fortified himself at breakfast with six eggs well beaten in a large bowl to the horror of a circle of aesthetic friends, stood his ground to the last.

Mrs. Stanton wrote later in her memoirs that the action of the Convention was the topic of discussion in public and private for a long time and stung many women into new thoughts and actions, thus giving rise to the movement for women's political equality, both in England and the United States.

26

After their honeymoon, the Stantons returned to America and stayed with Judge Cady in his house at Johnstown, where it was decided that Henry should enter his father-in-law's office and commence the study of law. In the autumn of 1853, the former was admitted to the bar and went into practice in Boston, which in those days happened to be the home of many of the leading men and women reformers, including William Lloyd Garrison.

Every year anti-slavery conventions were held in Boston, and the Stantons soon found themselves friends and intimates of those whom they had admired up to then at a distance. Only one thing Elizabeth regretted, and that was that she and Lucretia Mott had not met again since they parted in London, and that nothing further had yet been done about the Women's Rights Convention which they had planned.

Elizabeth's first son was born soon after their arrival in Johnstown and a second son followed in March, 1844, when they were in Boston. Although the intellectual climate of this town suited the Stantons, its severe winters affected Henry's health and, in the spring of 1847, they moved to Seneca Falls. Here they spent sixteen years of married life and other children, two sons and two daughters, were born. In Boston, all Elizabeth's immediate friends had been lively intellectuals and she had lived in the heart of the town, cared for by well-trained servants. Her new home in Seneca Falls was a house which had been empty for some years, set in five acres of grounds overgrown with weeds. It was badly in need of repair and was situated in an isolated position.

There were no sidewalks at this time and the roads were often very muddy. To make matters worse Henry was frequently away from home and the only servants she was able to engage were both lazy and incompetent. "I had so many cares that now I understood as never before the practical difficulties most married women had to contend with. No wonder they had such a weary, anxious look."

She felt strongly that some active measures should be taken to remedy all this. "My experience at the World's Anti-Slavery Convention, all I had read about the legal status of women, and the oppression I saw everywhere, together swept across my soul, intensified now by many personal experiences. It seemed as if all the elements had conspired to impel me to some onward step. I could not see what to do or where to begin—my only thought was a public meeting for protest and discussion."

Whilst she was in this condition of mind, Elizabeth received one morning a letter from Lucretia Mott to say that she was visiting friends not so many miles distant at Waterloo, and would she spend a day with her?

"There I met several members of different families of Friends, earnest, thoughtful women. I poured out the torrents of my long-accumulating discontent with such vehemence and indignation that I stirred myself, as well as the rest of the party, to do and dare anything. My discontent, according to Emerson, must have been healthy, for it moved us all to prompt action, and we decided, then and there, to call a Women's Rights Convention. We wrote the call that evening, and published it in the *Seneca County Courier* the next day, the fourteenth of July, 1848."

This is the announcement that appeared on that anniversary of the Fall of the Bastille:

"The first Women's Rights Convention to discuss the social, civil, and religious conditions and rights of women will be held in the Wesleyan chapel at Seneca Falls on Wednesday and Thursday current, commencing at ten a.m. During the first day, the meeting will be exclusively for women, who are earnestly invited to attend. The public generally are invited to be present on the second day when Lucretia Mott of Philadelphia will address the Convention." This was unsigned.

Never since Seneca Falls had come into existence in 1790, was there so much excitement among the inhabitants—such a fluttering of hearts among the fair sex—and by the way the men carried on, one would have thought they were fearing a raid by a tribe of scalp-hunting Red Indians instead of a visit from a mild Quaker lady and some of her friends. Already that year, less than three months previously and only a few miles away at Geneva, Miss Elizabeth Blackwell had caused a sensation through becoming admitted as a student to the Medical College.

On July 16th, the Sunday before the Convention, Lucretia and Elizabeth met with their chief supporters, Lucretia's sister, Mrs. Martha C. Wright, and a Miss Jane Hunt, in Mrs. Mary Ann McClintock's parlour to draw up a programme for the meeting. Unfortunately they had no experience in this sort of thing. They studied reports of the proceedings of various Temperance and Anti-Slavery Conventions to try to get guidance, but somehow the way these bodies conducted their conferences seemed too tame and conventional a model for launching a rebellion such as the world had never seen before.

After much delay, Mrs. Stanton had an inspiration. She suggested that they should use the Declaration of Independence of 1776 with some slight changes, such as substituting "All men" for "King George". The main task now was to find eighteen feminine grievances to replace those given in the original Declaration. A hurried search was made through statute books, church usages, and the customs of society to find that exact number. Several well-disposed men assisted in collecting grievances until, with the finding of the eighteenth, the women felt they had enough material to present a strong case before the world.

As it so happened, the first important step towards the improvement of a woman's status had been taken the previous year, thanks to the wealthy Dutch land-owners in the State of New York, who resented the idea of their property falling into the hands of dissolute sons-in-law, and gave their support to the Married Women's Property Bill, which made it legal for married women to hold real estate in their own name. But this applied only to the State of New York.

The eventful day dawned, and some in carriages and some on foot wended their way to the Chapel. Amongst them was Amelia Bloomer. The key was inserted in the lock, but the door refused to open. At last, a ladder was procured and a male sympathizer climbed in through a window and discovered that the door had been bolted on the inside by some would-be saboteur.

In filed the delegates, followed not only by the local ladies, but by many men as well. The latter had not been invited to the first day's proceedings, but as it was impossible for the women to eject them, they were allowed to remain. It was then hurriedly decided that in the circumstances it would be advisable if Lucretia's husband, the tall and dignified Quaker, James Mott, took the chair.

After Mrs. Mott in an impressive speech had des-cribed the humiliating condition of her sex all over the world, Mrs. Stanton read out the Declaration of Senti-ments. It had been a wise move on her part to use Thomas Jefferson's phrases, for they sounded even more pertinent when used in the cause of women.

"We hold these truths to be self-evident; that all men and women are created equal; that they are endowed by their Creator with certain inalienable rights; that among these are life, liberty, and the pursuit of happiness; that to secure these rights, governments are instituted, deriving their just powers from the consent of the governed.

"The history of mankind is a history of repeated injuries on the part of man towards woman, having in direct object the establishment of an absolute tyranny over her. To prove this, let facts be submitted to a candid world."

Mrs. Stanton then read out the eighteen grievances.

"He has never permitted her to exercise her inalienable right to the elective franchise.

"He has compelled her to submit to laws, in the formation of which she had no voice.

"He has withheld from her rights which are given to the most ignorant and degraded men—both natives and foreigners.

"Having deprived her of this first right of a citizen, the elective franchise, thereby leaving her without representation in the halls of legislation, he has oppressed her on all sides.

"He has made her, if married, in the eyes of the law, civilly dead.

"He has taken from her all rights in property, even to the wages she earns.

"He has made her, morally, an irresponsible being, as she can commit many crimes with impunity, provided they be done in the presence of her husband. In the covenant of marriage, she is compelled to promise obedience to her husband, he becoming, to all intents and purposes, her master—the law giving him power to deprive her of her liberty and to administer chastisement.

"He has so framed the laws of divorce, as to what shall be the proper causes, and in case of separation, to whom the guardianship of the children shall be given, as to be wholly regardless of the happiness of women— the law, in all cases, going upon a false supposition of the supremacy of men, and giving all power into his hands.

"After depriving her of all rights as a married woman, if single and the owner of property, he has taxed her to support a government which recognizes her only when her property can be made profitable to it.

"He has monopolized all the profitable employments, and from those she is permitted to follow, she receives but a scanty remuneration. He closes against her all the avenues to wealth and distinction which he considers most honourable to himself. As a leader of theology, medicine, or law, she is not known.

"He has denied the facilities for obtaining a thorough education, all colleges being closed against her.

"He allows her in Church, as well as State, but a subordinate position, claiming Apostolic authority for her exclusion from the ministry, and with some exceptions, from any public participation in the affairs of the Church.

"He has created a false, public sentiment by giving to the world a different code of morals for men and women, by which the moral delinquencies which exclude women from society are not only tolerated, but deemed of little account in man.

"He has usurped the prerogative of Jehovah himself, claiming it as his right to assign to her a sphere of action, when that belongs to her conscience and to her God.

"He has endeavoured in every way that he could to destroy her confidence in her own powers, to lessen her self-respect, and to make her willing to lead a dependent and abject life.

"Now, in view of this entire disfranchisement of one-half the people of this country, their social and religious degradation—in view of the unjust laws above mentioned, and because women do feel themselves aggrieved, oppressed, and fraudulently deprived of their most sacred rights, we insist that they have immediate admission to all the rights and privileges which belong to them as citizens of the United States.

"In entering upon the great work before us, we anticipate no small amount of misconception, misrepresentation, and ridicule, but we shall use every instrumentality within our power to effect our object. We shall employ agents, circulate tracts, petition the State and National Legislatures, and endeavour to enlist the Pulpit and the Press in our behalf."

Mrs. Stanton spoke clearly and effectively, and her fellow delegates nodded their approval when she sat down to great applause.

What an attractive-looking woman, thought Amelia Bloomer from her seat in the middle of the chapel. Her eyes dwelt on Mrs. Stanton's healthy red cheeks and bobbing black curls. Though she did not speak herself, she listened with growing interest to the lively discussion that followed. She wanted to talk it all over with Dexter first before committing herself. But of one thing she was certain, she liked Mrs. Stanton and admired her sincerity and courage.

On the Thursday, the chapel could have been filled twice over with the curious and the hostile. But, by arriving early through a side door, the delegates and their sympathizers were able to pack the hall and prevent the entry of any trouble-makers.

The resolutions of the Declaration of Sentiments were each in turn, posed, debated, and then passed without a single dissident vote. When they had come to the end, to the astonishment and consternation of her fellow delegates, Elizabeth rose and announced that she had her own further resolution to propose. Elizabeth was fully aware that what she was about to say would be regarded by many as beyond all reason, but she had never forgotten the advice the Irish liberator, Daniel O'Connell, had given her in London. "Remember this," he had stressed. "It is always good policy to claim the uttermost, then you will be sure to get something!"

And so, on July 20th, 1848, in the Wesleyan Chapel at Seneca Falls, Elizabeth claimed the uttermost for her sex. "Resolved that it is the duty of the women of this country to secure for themselves the sacred right to the elective franchise." She pleaded for this with fervour and persuasive skill, but when she had finished she feared that no one would second her resolution. She looked about her. Would nobody rise to support her?

Amelia looked questioningly at Dexter, but he shook his head. Then a man, the Negro Abolitionist, Frederick Douglass, stood up and spoke with such eloquence for the resolution that when put to the vote, it was passed by a small majority. But Mr. Douglass was an exception. Most men were against giving women the vote, and seventy-two years elapsed before they were granted it in the United States.

Tremendous publicity was given to the Convention by all the newspapers. It was the first time anywhere in the world that women had dared to openly rebel against their lot and hold such a meeting. And what was

34

even more alarming, they planned a whole series of Conventions to be held all over the country!

"Insurrection Among Women!" "The Reign of Petticoats!" ran the headlines. The organizers of the Convention were stated to be a rebellious group of aged spinsters, crossed in love, trying to avenge themselves and make others more miserable than themselves. Their secret aim, it was alleged, was to relegate men to the kitchen while they swaggered about the world. The Press ignored the fact that both Lucretia and Elizabeth were married women, and that the latter was already the mother of three boys.

Only Horace Greeley in the *New York Tribune* wrote a sympathetic editorial on the subject. "It is easy to be smart, to be droll, to be facetious in opposition to the demands of these Female Reformers, and in decrying assumptions so novel and opposed to established habit and usages, a little wit will go a great way. But when a sincere republican is asked to say in sober earnest what adequate reason he can give for refusing the demand of women to an equal participation with men in political rights, he must answer, none at all."

Elizabeth read everything that appeared in the papers. She was delighted at the publicity they were receiving. "It will start women thinking—and men, too," she wrote to a friend, "and when men and women think about a new problem, the first step in progress is taken. The great fault of mankind is that it will not think."

She countered attacks in the Press by writing in reply letters both spirited in style and loaded with facts. Occasionally she delivered a lecture to interested societies and organizations in the State of New York. A great believer in physical exercise as a means of keeping children out of mischief, she started up a gymnasium with a German instructor. Looking ahead into the future, when she confidently believed that women would have equal rights with men, she did all in her power to prepare the local school girls for such a life. When lessons ended in the afternoon, she would be waiting at the Academy gate to march all those she could persuade to the gymnasium, where they were taught the same physical exercises as the boys. Meanwhile at home, in order to eradicate any ideas of sex superiority in her sons, she made them wait at table when they had guests, a service for which she paid them.

And how did Mrs. Bloomer regard the activities of this extraordinary woman who had come to live in her small town? She had liked her when she had seen her for the first time at the Convention, but, influenced by Dexter, she had decided that Mrs. Stanton had gone too far in demanding the vote for women, and consequently had not put her name to the Declaration of Sentiments.

Nevertheless, the content of the Declaration began to have an effect upon her thoughts and actions, as it did upon those of many other women of that day. It brought to their attention in a dramatic way the fact that the laws of their country were heavily weighted against them, and that they themselves must take the initiative and fight to restore the balance.

In Seneca Falls, one of the first results of this new outlook was the formation of a Ladies Temperance Society, of which Amelia Bloomer was an officer. She wrote in her journal that up to then, "We had almost no part in all this temperance work. Women could attend meetings and listen to the eloquence and arguments of men, but such a thing as their having anything to say or do further than this was not thought of."

36

Later, it was decided that the new Society must have a paper of its own. The ladies were encouraged by a temperance lecturer who was touring the States. He promised to find them subscribers and money during his travels. He sent them lists of names and addresses, but no money. They never heard from him again. But, undismayed by this, they carried on with their plans and Mrs. Bloomer was appointed Editor, though her husband stressed the risks of the venture. He said that it would cost a lot of money, and that they would get into debt, but the ladies were determined and ignored his advice. And so, on January 1st, 1849, *The Lily* was launched.

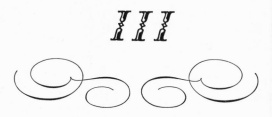

III

THE LILY

"I NEVER LIKED the name of the paper," Mrs. Bloomer has recorded, "but the Society thought it pretty and accepted it from the President. It started with that name, and became known far and wide. It had been baptized with tears and sent forth with anxious doubts and fears. It was not easy to change, and so it remained *The Lily* to the end, pure in its motive and purpose as in name."

During the initial year of its existence, the paper had printed at the top of its front page the words, "Published by a Committee of Ladies". But in fact no one, except Mrs. Bloomer, had any part in the running of it. Consequently, in January, 1850, the heading was changed to the words, "Devoted to the Interests of Women", and Mrs. Bloomer's name alone appeared as publisher and editor.

The front page of the first number of *The Lily* is reproduced as one of the illustrations to this book. This copy was once Mrs. Bloomer's personal property and it is interesting to note that, with pardonable pride, she has crossed out the words, "Published by a Committee of Ladies", and has written her own name in substitution.

About three hundred copies were printed of the opening issue and, despite Dexter's misgivings, the paper paid its way and its circulation steadily increased. It was an exciting new life for Amelia. She learnt how to correct proofs, how to compose attractively worded circulars to try to gain new subscribers, how to write editorials and become expert in all the other work of an editor.

"*The Lily* was the first paper published and devoted to the interests of women," she claimed in later life, "and, so far as I know, the first one owned, edited, and published by a woman."

In the spring of 1849, in recognition of his work in support of the successful party in the elections, Mr. Bloomer was appointed Postmaster of Seneca Falls. Impressed by the success his wife was making of *The Lily,* and in amends for his earlier discouragement, he proposed that Amelia should act as his deputy. She accepted the position as she had determined to give a practical demonstration "of woman's right to fill any place for which she had capacity". She was sworn in and held the office for the following four years. "Many thought I was out of woman's sphere, but the venture was very successful, and proved to me conclusively that a woman might engage in any respectable business and deal with all sorts of men, and yet be treated with the utmost respect and consideration."

Something else happened that spring—something which had the ultimate effect of making Amelia throw aside her doubts about the expediency of the Declaration of Sentiments—and come out in support of it. The Legislature of Tennessee, after gravely debating the

39

question, had decided that women had no souls and therefore no right to own property.

Roused to anger by this insult to her sex, Mrs. Bloomer in her editorial for the month of March wrote, "Wise men these, and worthy to be honoured with seats in the halls of legislation in a Christian land. Women no souls! Then, of course, we are not accountable beings, and if not accountable to our Maker, then surely not to man. Man represents, legislates for us, and now holds himself accountable for us! How kind in him, and what a weight is lifted from us! We shall no longer be answerable to the laws of God or man, no longer be subject to punishment for breaking them, no longer be responsible for any of our doings. Man in whom iniquity is perfected has assumed the whole charge of us and left us helpless, soulless, defenceless creatures dependent on him for leave to speak or act.

"We suppose the wise legislators consider the question settled beyond dispute, but we fear they will have some trouble with it yet. Although it may be an easy matter for them to arrive at such a conclusion, it will be quite another thing to make women believe it. We are not so blind to the weakness and imperfection of man as to set his word above that of our Maker, or so ready to yield obedience to his laws as to place them before the laws of God. However blindly we may be led by them, however much we may yield to his acquired power over us, we cannot yet fall down and worship him as our superior. Some men even act as though women had no souls, but it remained for the legislature of Tennessee to speak it to the world.

"We have not designed *ourself* saying much on the subject of Women's Rights; but we feel here so much that is calculated to keep our sex down and impress us with a conviction of our inferiority and helplessness, that we feel compelled to act on the defensive and stand for what we consider our just rights. If things are coming to such a pass as that indicated by the above decision, we think it high time that women should open their eyes and look where they stand. It is quite time that their rights *should be discussed,* and that woman herself should enter the contest.

"We have ever felt that in regard to property, and also as to many other things, the laws were unjust to women. Men make laws without consulting us, and of course they will make them all in their own favour, especially as we are powerless and cannot contend for our rights.

"We believe that most women are capable of taking care of their own property, that they have the right to hold it, and should dispose of it as they please, man's decision to the contrary not withstanding. As for ourselves, we have no fears but we could take care of a fortune if we had one, without any assistance from legislators or lawyers, and we should think them meddling with what did not concern them should they undertake to control it for us.

"The law of our own State has taken a step in advance on this subject and granted to women the right to their own property. We trust this is but a forecast of the enlightened sentiments of the people of New York, and that it will pave the way to greater privileges, and the final elevation of woman to that position in society which shall entitle her opinion to respect and consideration."

It is clear from this editorial that Mrs. Bloomer was extremely put out by the suggestion that she did not possess a soul. From that time on, a considerable part of *The Lily* was devoted to the same subject. The effect of all this was to make her more aggressively a feminist, and soon she was demanding in her columns the right of suffrage so that her sex should possess a controlling influence in the passage of all laws.

She claimed that she had always been at heart in sympathy with the Declaration of Sentiments. She recollected how, when in her teens, her feelings had been deeply stirred by learning that an old lady, a dear friend, was to be turned out of her home and the bulk of her property taken from her. Her husband had died suddenly leaving no will. The law would allow her but a life interest in one third of the estate, which had been accumulated by the joint savings of herself and husband through many years. They had no children and the nearest relative of the husband was a third cousin, and to him the law gave two-thirds of her property, though he had never contributed a dollar towards its accumulation and was to them a stranger.

Anxious to propagate her ideas amongst the local ladies, Amelia now comfortably furnished a small room next to the Post Office, where they could exchange views and read the periodicals that came to her as editor of *The Lily*—and study the six pages of the latter if their husbands forbade them to be subscribers.

A frequent visitor was the plump, jolly-looking matron—scarcely five foot high—Mrs. Elizabeth Cady Stanton. It was not long before she was writing articles for *The Lily* under the pseudonym of "Sun Flower". She was now the mother of a fourth son. This infant was eighteen months old in the summer of 1850, when his eldest brother, Henry, invented a life preserver made out of cork. Accompanied by a troop of expectant boys, the baby was drawn in his carriage to the banks of the river, stripped, the string of corks tied under his arms, and set afloat. The inventor and his young friends followed in a rowing-boat. The baby, accustomed to a morning bath in a large tub, splashed about joyfully, keeping his head above water. He was as blue as indigo and as cold as a frog when rescued by his mother.

The next day the same infant was seen by a passer-by seated on a chimney on the highest peak of the roof of the Stantons' home. Without alarming anyone, this man climbed up and rescued the child. These were typical examples of the tranquillity Mrs. Stanton said she enjoyed during her first years of motherhood.

With such a background of domestic cares, it is not surprising that "Sun Flower's" first contribution to *The Lily* should have been an attack on sewing, which she called a worthless and unhealthy employment, a dead loss to the one who did it. "As an amusement, it is contemptible; as an educator of head or heart, worthless; as a developer of muscles, of no avail; as a support, the most miserably paid of trades. It is a continued drain on sight and strength, on health and life, and it should be the study of every woman to do as little of it as possible."

Elizabeth acknowledged that some sewing should be done, but demanded that it should be cut to a minimum. "What use is all the flummery, puffing, and mysterious folding we see in ladies' dresses? What use in ruffles on round pillow cases, night caps, and children's clothes? What use in making shirts for our lords in the wonderful manner we now do, with all those tiny plaits, and rows of stitching down before, and round the collars and wrist bands? Why, all these things are done to make men, children, women, chairs, sofas and tables look pretty! If women for the last fifty years had spent all the time they have wasted on furbelowing their rags, in riding, walking, and playing on the lawn with their children, the whole race would look ten times as well as they now do!"

To the consternation of many, Mrs. Stanton

advocated that everyone should do his or her own sewing, or leave it "to that class especially fitted for it, those idle men who lounge about stores and on street corners, whittling and talking away the hours". She had already taught her own boys sewing, so she was practising what she preached when she went on: "We must see that boys are early taught to sew. Seriously, I see no reason why boys should be left to roam the streets day and night, wholly unemployed, a nuisance to everybody and a curse to themselves, while their sisters are overtaxed at home to make and mend their brothers' clothes. It will be a glorious day for the emancipation of those of our sex who have long been slaves to the needle, when men and boys make their own clothes, and women make theirs in the plainest possible manner."

In another article she suggested a change in the way women fastened their clothes. "From the general fashion of their garments, persons of the middle classes and even servants, are continually obliged to seek assistance in dressing. Hardly a dressmaker is willing to make dresses open in front. How absurd! We never see men having any fashion which makes it necessary to fasten any part of their garments at the back. They are not so foolish. All classes, rich and poor, should be able to put off and on their own clothing readily and without assistance."

Mrs. Bloomer herself became infected by her lively contributor's unconventional outlook, and in one editorial she startled her readers by querying the custom for women to be known by their husbands' names and titles. "Why a woman as soon as she is married is willing to drop the good name of Mary or Elizabeth and take that of John, Thomas or Harry, I never could understand. And as for titles, why should a woman be called Mrs. General, Mrs. Colonel, Mrs. Captain, or Mrs. Judge, I do not know, except it be on the principle that husband and wife are one, and that one the husband, and the wife is his appendage and must be known by his title instead of having an individuality of her own.

"So far is this matter of appropriating names and titles carried, that women retain them after the death of their husbands and call themselves Mrs. Colonel or Mrs. Doctor when there is no such Doctor or Colonel in existence. When a man is dead, his title should die with him, and his wife should assume her own Christian name.

"The name or title of her husband gives no additional dignity or character to her, and it sinks her own individuality in him; which no woman should allow.

"Adam named his wife Eve, and we have no account of her ever being called Mrs. Adam. Victoria of England has never called herself Mrs. Albert Saxe-Coburg, nor has Eugénie been known as Mrs. Emperor Louis Napoleon. All married Queens, all married women of any distinction have ever been known by their Christian names. The wife of our first President is known as Martha Washington, instead of Mrs. George Washington.

"May the day soon come when women bear honoured titles of their own, earned and conferred, but not borrowed."

The tone of *The Lily* was changing; it was becoming more forthright, more militant. "The Emancipation of Woman from Intemperance, Injustice, Prejudice, and Bigotry" was now printed beneath the title. Those who met Amelia for the first time after having read her editorials were astonished by her mild appearance. She seemed so very amiable with her chubby cheeks and her soft reddish-brown hair. Only the fire that sometimes flashed into her blue eyes hinted that there might be another side to her personality.

45

She could be outspoken when publishing reasons for rejecting unsuitable contributions. " 'To the Boys of Seneca' is declined. Try your hand at writing prose, friend, before you attempt to be a poet." " 'Indignant' would better effect her object should she address her lines directly to the person for whom they are intended through the Post Office. They cannot appear in *The Lily*." " 'Tight Waist Dress'—this is a good subject, but the article before us is not written with sufficient care. It needs altering and punctuating; and this we have not time to do."

She would always quote in *The Lily* any reports she might come across in other papers of injustices to women, such as the following from the *Westminster Review* of London: "A lady whose husband had been unsuccessful in business established herself as a milliner in Manchester. After some years of toil, she realized sufficient for the family to live upon comfortably, the husband having done nothing meanwhile. They lived for a time in easy circumstances after she gave up business, and then the husband died bequeathing all his wife's earnings to his illegitimate children. At the age of 62, she was compelled, in order to gain her bread, to return to business."

She was always quick to defend her sex against attack in the Press, even when they were doing something of which she herself disapproved. Two fashionable ladies who dared to promenade down Fulton Street smoking cigars came in for much scathing comment. "Surely we have an equal right to it?" Mrs. Bloomer commented in *The Lily*. "The idea has too long existed that man may degrade and debase himself by the vilest practices, and yet be respected, while woman is forbidden to step beyond the bounds which he has set, under penalty of having her character destroyed and

46

her happiness blasted for ever. We wish to see some reform in this respect. We would by no means have our sex follow the bad example set them by the 'lords of creation', but we would have them shun and despise what they would condemn in us."

By 1851, when *The Lily* entered upon its third year, its circulation had steadily risen to some five hundred copies a month and all the leading feminists were now regular contributors to its pages. Then something happened which brought the little paper world-wide notoriety, and made its circulation soar—so that by 1853, it was appearing not once but twice a month, and selling over four thousand copies an issue.

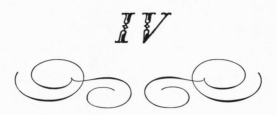

PETTICOATS AND TIGHT LACING

IN THE middle of the nineteenth century most women's skirts trailed on the ground, and some gowns took between twenty and thirty yards of material to make. When the Crystal Palace was built in 1851 for the Great Exhibition, the architect, Joseph Paxton, thought that it would be very difficult to keep the floors clean, so he invented a machine to do the work and the authorities, at great expense, had several of these manufactured. But they were never used, because the floors of the Crystal Palace were kept swept and polished by the ladies' trains!

Beneath her long skirts the average woman would wear many undergarments. First one would probably find a white cambric petticoat with a border of *broderie anglaise*. Under this might be a plain white longcloth petticoat—then a flannel petticoat, followed by another flannel petticoat, both with scalloped hems. Next would come a petticoat, lined and corded with horsehair, which had a straw plait six feet long in its hem to make it stand out. Last of all, the lace-trimmed drawers.

48

There were variations on this, of course. Three starched muslin petticoats, some of them flounced, might replace the flannel ones in very hot weather. Some ladies wore a wheel of thick plaited horsehair just below the waist to diminish its apparent size and make their gowns stand well away from their figures. These were known as "deceivers".

In a book of household hints, written in the form of questions and answers, and popular in 1851, occurs the following question, "Why are flannels superior in comfort and benefit to any other materials for underclothing?"

The answer reads: "Because they possess in an eminent degree non-conducting and absorbent properties. By the first property, they prevent the heat within the body from escaping too abruptly and thereby causing chills, and secondly they exclude the cold air from contacting with the surface, preventing colds and coughs, etc. Flannel is a good sanitary agent when worn next to the skin because the nap or pile on the flannel keeps up a constant degree of mild irritation on the cuticle, acting as a detergent or cleaner of the skin, and, by keeping open the pores, answers the purpose of a gentle flesh-brush."

Never had woman carried such a quantity of materials on her person. It is said that a tulle dress of four skirts, ruched, made for the Empress Eugénie took one thousand one hundred yards of material. The secretary of the American Treasury reported in 1851 that among the importations from Europe were lace, silks, worsteds, veils, and satins to the value of $23,649,341.

Under her bodice a lady wore a camisole to protect the dress from the stays. The latter were formidable pieces of armour which had been growing in length by degrees. A writer of the period wrote that the gait of the average fashionable lady was stiff and awkward on account of the form of her stays. Others considered that tight-lacing assisted a lady to attain that pose of passive immobility which was so much admired at that time. No lady thus attired could stoop to conquer. A papa of the period describes what happened when his daughter was rash enough to stoop. "Her stays gave way with a tremendous explosion, and she fell to the ground. I thought she had snapped in two."

An article on stays in *The Ladies' Cabinet*, a fashion magazine, quotes a conversation attributed to an eminent surgeon, whose strong sense and great love of truth frequently carried him beyond the bounds of politeness even with the female sex. A lady of high rank complained to him of certain internal pains and disagreeable sensations she could not in any way account for.

"Madam," he replied, "it is your damned stays. We are just like bladders half filled with wind and water. If we press too hard upon one part, the contents must overflow another. Leave off your stays—take my pills —and you'll soon be better, if you mind what I say."

Many women wore pointed stays emphasizing a long waist; the bodice was form-fitting and held the arms in such a position that it was impossible to raise them.

Another critic of tight-lacing compared three customs —that of the savage Indian who changed the shape of the soft and elastic bones of the skull of its infant by compressing it between two boards; that of the intelligent, but prejudiced Chinese who confined the feet of females to the size of an infant's; and that of the cultured and well-informed white lady who limited the growth of her waist by the pressure of the stays.

He concluded, "When we consider the importance of the organs which suffer by these customs, surely we must acknowledge that the last is the most barbarous practice of the three."

Yet another critic of tight-lacing remarked: "No woman who dresses tightly can have good shoulders, a straight spine, good lungs, sweet breath, and be perfectly healthy."

In an attack on corsets in a ladies' magazine, the writer painted a lurid picture of this instrument of torture "trammelling a woman's genteel thorax with springs of steel and whalebone, screwing in the waist to Death's hour-glass contraction, and squeezing lungs, liver, and midriff into an unutterable cram."

In the next issue: "An Old Subscriber" wrote anonymously in defence of corsets. She could easily understand that a girl, who was full grown and who had been unaccustomed to wear tight stays, should find it difficult and painful to lace in her waist to a fashionable size. She suggested, however, that if the corset be worn at an early age and the figure gradually moulded by it, no terrible consequences need be feared. She would therefore recommend the early use of a corset that fitted the figure nicely and no more, which would in a great measure prevent the waist of a growing girl from becoming clumsy.

If, however, on her reaching the age of fourteen, her waist still be considered too large, a smaller corset might be worn with advantage, which should be gradually tightened till the requisite slimness was achieved. Our "Old Subscriber" claimed that she knew of so many cases where under this system girls had, when full grown, possessed both a good figure and good health, that she could recommend it with confidence to those parents who wished their children to grow up into elegant and healthy women. She claimed that many of the

51

strongest and healthiest women she had seen in London Society were tight-lacers.

This defence of stays would hardly convince a modern miss, yet stays did at least prevent ladies of the period from getting slipped discs!

The hampering weight of the numerous petticoats worn in the 1850s undoubtedly restricted swift movement. With so many bulky underclothes, it is not surprising perhaps that women tight-laced, for otherwise their waist measurements might have been over thirty inches.

Various ingenious alternatives to a plethora of petticoats were put on the market from time to time, such as the "*Jupon Ballon*" or "Balloon Petticoat" with tubes attached round its hem. These the wearer got her maid to inflate each morning before the ritual of dressing. The idea was a good one, but in practice it somehow did not prove too successful. For Lady Aylesbury, one designer invented a single quilted petticoat for her to wear. This was filled with eiderdown and swelled out to an enormous expanse whenever milady sat or rose, and made her dress float like a vast cloud. This petticoat caused quite a stir, but it was not destined to become popular for apart from the expense, it was hardly the thing to wear in warm weather.

It is clear that many women felt handicapped by their clothes and would welcome a change of fashion. Such was the position when the Bloomer appeared.

When Dexter C. Bloomer became Postmaster, he disposed of his interest in *The Seneca County Courier*. The new editor was a conservative gentleman who had no sympathy with the feminist cause, and had annoyed Mrs. Bloomer on more than one occasion by his patronizing editorials in which he had reproved her for beating the rub-a-dub of agitation in *The Lily*.

In January, 1851, he commented in *The Courier* on the report from London, England, that in that city "improvement in the attire of females was being agitated". He went on to observe that many inconveniences, many a shock to a delicate lady, might be obviated by the adoption of a less cumbersome mode of attire than currently fashionable. Then, with his tongue in his cheek, he suggested a change to Turkish pantaloons and a skirt reaching a little below the knee.

This article gave Mrs. Bloomer an opportunity to score off her critic. In her next issue, she congratulated him on having gone so far ahead of her as to advocate women wearing pantaloons. She wrote in a half-serious, half-playful style. In the following week's *Courier* he expressed surprise that she should treat so important a matter with levity.

Amelia immediately returned to the attack in *The Lily*, saying that she was glad to learn that he was serious in his proposal. "Had we broached this subject, the cry would have been raised on all sides, 'She wants to wear pantaloons', and a pretty hornet's nest we should have got into. But now that our cautious editor of *The Courier* recommends it, we suppose that there will be no harm in our doing so. Small waists and whalebones can be dispensed with, and we shall be allowed breathing-room; and our forms shall be what nature made them. We are so thankful that men are beginning to undo some of the mischief they have done us."

Mrs. Bloomer, of course, was aware that already in England Helen Marie Weber—that extraordinary woman who ploughed her own land during the day and sat up half the night writing with vigour in favour of women's rights—wore as her everyday apparel a black coat and pantaloons and, for best, a dark-blue dress coat with gilt buttons, a buff cassimore waistcoat and dun-coloured trousers. She was aware, too, that Mrs. Weber had written: "Those who suppose that women can be the political, social, pecuniary, religious equal of man without conforming to his dress, are deceiving themselves. While the superiority of the male dress for all purposes of business and recreation is conceded, it is absurd to argue that we should not avail ourselves of its advantages."

In a letter to an American friend in 1850, Mrs. Weber prophesied that within ten years male attire would be widely worn by women all over the world, and that many social reforms would follow.

Amelia at that time had certainly not been in favour of women wearing pantaloons. Indeed, Mrs. Stanton, too, had been against it and had written in the June, 1850, issue of *The Lily*: "As to their costume, the gents need have no fear of our imitating them, for we think it is in violation of every principle of duty, taste, and dignity; and, notwithstanding the contempt and abuse cast upon our loose garments, we still admire their easy graceful folds."

But Elizabeth Cady Stanton's attitude was to change completely in the February of the following year. Not as the result of *The Courier* versus *The Lily* controversy, but owing to a visit from Cousin Libby, following her Grand Tour of Europe.

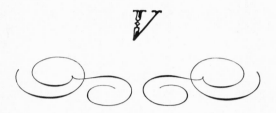

THE BIRTH OF THE BLOOMER

COUSIN LIBBY was the daughter of Gerrit Smith, a prominent politician who had inherited a fortune from his father, Pete Smith, a fur trader beloved of the Indians. Gerrit was a liberal-minded man, who lived in a simply furnished house in which he would have nothing that might make his poorest guest feel ill at ease. He was a practical Christian who modelled his life on the belief that God had given him money to give away, and so he parted with most of the land he had inherited to the needy.

Judge Cady regarded Gerrit as a dangerous radical and disapproved of the way he brought up Libby to romp and play like a boy. Her father held that as long as women went on wearing cumbersome, crippling clothes, they would enjoy no status higher than that of slaves. He encouraged Libby to dress as she pleased, donning nothing that might injure her health or interfere with her comfort or the free and easy motion of her limbs.

In 1850, Libby married Charles Dudley Miller and

55

went for her honeymoon on the Grand Tour of Europe. Whilst in Switzerland she had made for herself an all-purpose travelling costume, similar in design to what was worn in sanatoria there by women recuperating from the effects of tight-lacing and lack of physical exercise. This consisted of long, full Turkish trousers of black broadcloth and a short skirt reaching just below the knee. For outdoor wear, she added a Spanish cloak of the same material, dark furs and a beaver hat trimmed with feathers. Her husband thoroughly approved of this outfit and defended his pioneering wife against all criticism. She was thus dressed when she came to stay with her cousin in Seneca Falls.

Elizabeth Cady Stanton was delighted with the costume. In her old age, she wrote that to see Libby with a lamp in one hand and the latest Stanton baby in the other, walk upstairs with ease and grace, whilst she with flowing robes pulled herself up with difficulty, carrying only a can of hot water, convinced her that there was sore need of reform in women's dress. So she promptly made herself a similar costume.

A few days later, one freezing February morning, the two cousins strolled happily along the main street of Seneca Falls in their rational dress to the consternation of the inhabitants. "Like a captive set free from his ball and chain," avowed Mrs. Stanton, "I was always ready for a brisk walk throught sleet and snow and rain, to climb a mountain, jump over a fence, work in the garden, and was fit for any necessary locomotion. What a sense of liberty I felt with no skirts to hold or brush, ready at any moment to climb a hill-top to see the sun go down or the moon rise, with no ruffles or trails limped by the dew or soiled by the grass."

And how did Mrs. Bloomer react when they called at the Post Office?

Let her speak for herself. "Having taken part in the discussion of the dress question, it seemed proper that I should practise as I preached, and as the *Courier* man advised, and so, a few days later, I, too, donned the new costume. And in the next issue of my paper announced that fact to my readers. At the outset, I had no idea of fully adopting the style; no thought of setting a fashion; no thought that my action would create an excitement throughout the civilized world, and give to the style my name and the credit due to Mrs. Miller. This was all the work of the Press. I stood amazed at the furore I had unwittingly caused. The *New York Tribune* contained the first notice I saw of my action. Other papers caught it up and handed it about. Some praised and some blamed, some ridiculed and condemned.

" 'Bloomerism', 'Bloomerite', and 'Bloomers' were the headings of many an article, item and squib; and finally someone—I don't know to whom I am indebted for the honour—wrote the 'Bloomer Costume' and the name has continued to cling to the short dress, in spite of my repeatedly disclaiming all right to it and giving Mrs. Miller's name as that of the originator and the first to wear such a dress in public. Had she not come to us in that style, it is not probable that either Mrs. Stanton or myself would have donned it."

As soon as it became known that Mrs. Bloomer was wearing the new dress, letters came pouring in upon her from women all over the country, asking for patterns and precise details of how to make it. It showed, Mrs. Bloomer recorded, how ready and anxious women were to throw off the burden of long, heavy skirts. It seemed as though half of the letters that came to the Post Office were for her.

To save herself a great deal of correspondence, Amelia described the dress in *The Lily*. "We would

57

have the skirt reaching down to a little below the knee, and not made quite so full as is the present fashion. Underneath this skirt, trousers made moderately full, in fair mild weather, coming down to the ankle (not instep) and there gathered in with an elastic band, or, what we think decidedly prettier, gathered three or four times, half an inch apart, and drawn up to just sufficient width to permit the foot to pass through. The shoes or slippers to suit the occasion. For winter or wet weather, the trousers also full, but coming down into a boot, which should rise at least three or four inches above the ankle. This boot should be gracefully sloped at the upper edge and trimmed with fur, or fancifully embroidered, according to the taste of the wearer. The material might be cloth, morocco, mooseskin, and so forth, and made waterproof if desirable."

In subsequent issues of her paper she enlarged on the subject. She told her readers that she and her friends made their dress with a loose and easy waist and without whalebone. Some made the dress with a sack front from shoulder to the knee, a tight back, and confined round the waist by a belt, sash, or cord and tassels. Others made it with a yoke at the neck and wore no bodice beneath. Each reader should be guided by her own taste and judgment in the matter. Shawls must be abandoned and a sacque or mantilla take their place. A nice round hat, Mrs. Bloomer suggested, would make the whole outfit unique.

Amelia and Mrs. Stanton had their daguerreotypes taken, and these were reproduced in the September issue of *The Lily*, with the following comments from the Editress. "We are not ambitious to show our face to our readers; all we seek is to let them see what an 'immodest' dress we are wearing, and about which people have made such an ado. We hope that our lady readers will not be shocked at our 'masculine' appearance, or gentlemen mistake us for one of their own sex."

Mrs. Stanton wrote an impassioned plea, urging all sensible women to follow their example. "We say to you, at your fireside, ladies, unhook your dresses, and let everything hang loosely about you. Now, take a long breath, swell out as far as you can, and at that point fasten your clothes. Now please cut off those flowing skirts to your knees, and put on a pair of loose trousers buttoned about your ankle. Let us correct our garments, until they assume their proper place; all standing out of the way of the full and perfect development of the woman!"

A fashionable lady of Seneca Falls wrote an outraged letter of protest to *The Lily* after reading this. Mrs. Bloomer replied in the next number: "Mrs. W.R.P. is advised that we occupy a position too high above her standard to be hurt by her ill-bred remarks. Had we not some regard for the feelings of her near friends, we would comply with her request and publish the note from her, with her signature, that our citizens might know how vulgar a mind dwells beneath a rich outward adornment."

Many others disapproved, of course. Judge Cady was very angry when he learnt that his daughter had been seen wearing a short skirt of black satin that ended just above her knees, over trousers of the same material. He wrote to Elizabeth that no woman of good sense and delicacy would make a "guy" of herself, and that he hoped she would not come to see him at his home at Johnstown thus attired.

Mrs. Stanton's eldest boy, who was at a progressive school, wrote to his mother also asking her not to wear the Bloomer costume when she visited him. And Mamma replied, "You do not wish me to visit you in a short

59

dress. Why, my dear child, I have no other. Now suppose you and I were taking a long walk in the fields and I had on three long petticoats. Then suppose a bull should take after us, why you with your arms and legs free, could run like a shot, but I, alas, should fall a victim to my graceful flowing drapery. My petticoats would be caught by the stumps and the briars, and what could I do at the fences? Then you in your agony, when you saw the bull gaining on me, would say, 'Oh, how I wish mother could use her legs as I can!' Now why do you wish me to wear what is uncomfortable, inconvenient, and many times dangerous? I'll tell you why. You want me to be like other people. You do not like to have me laughed at. You must learn not to care for what foolish people say. Such good men as Cousin Gerrit and Mr. Weld will tell you that a short dress is the right kind. So no matter if ignorant silly persons laugh."

Henry Stanton, recently elected to the Senate, thoroughly approved of his wife's new look. He was away from home in Albany when he first heard about it. "How does Lib Miller look in her new Turkish dress?" he wrote. "The worst about it would be, I should think, sitting down. Then ladies will expose their legs somewhat above the knee, to the delight of those gentlemen who are anxious to know whether their lady friends have round and plump legs, or lean and scrawny ones."

Elizabeth's brother-in-law was at first in the camp of her critics, but as time passed became resigned to her mannish mode and invited Libby and her to stay with him.

"You and Mrs. Miller can keep each other in countenance, whenever you wish to promenade Broadway in 'shorts'. The novelty of seeing a Bloomer in New York is so effectually worn off that I hear of no more insults or annoyance being offered to such as choose to wear the costume. So please pack up your coats and trousers and come along."

The invitation was gladly accepted. Realizing the importance of creating a good impression, the two women made themselves Bloomer costumes out of the very best materials, adorning them with lace. They were helped by Amelia, who after their departure anxiously awaited news of their reception in New York. At last the promised letter was delivered at the Post Office.

"I have been several days in the metropolis, have walked the streets, ridden in the omnibus, etc., and have met nothing unpleasant," wrote Mrs. Stanton. "The people look at us to be sure, but that is nothing. We went over to New Jersey on Saturday. The Ferry Boats and depôts were crowded, but not one disrespectful word was said. We have been taken for Hungarians. We all went to church yesterday and were treated with marked politeness. The talk about it being dangerous to walk the streets in the new costume, all humbug!"

She enjoyed her stay. There was no need for her to worry about what was happening at her home in Seneca Falls, for it was now being most expertly run by a young Quaker housekeeper, Amelia Willard. In later years Elizabeth was to write this testimonial in praise of her: "She was a treasure, a friend and comforter, a second mother to my children, who understood all life's duties and gladly bore its burdens. She could fill any department in domestic life, and for thirty years was the joy of our household. But for this noble, self-sacrificing woman, much of my public work would have been impossible."

Encouraged by the fact that she had not been stoned in the streets of New York, as her father had prophesied,

Mrs. Stanton made herself a white satin Bloomer costume with a loose waist, and went to a ball in it. "Henry and I danced until four o'clock. Everybody said I looked well, and I thought I did." She felt not in the least way fatigued, and this she attributed to the loose waist—"the most glorious part of the reform".

Then came Independence Day, and in the newspapers describing the celebrations held all over the country on that occasion, Mrs. Stanton and Mrs. Bloomer were to read some very encouraging reports.

At a ball in Akron, Ohio, over sixty of the ladies had been dressed in full Bloomer Costume. The *Cleveland Plaindealer* described the scene as enchanting. "Long dresses hitherto hid from view all the graceful movements of the lady dancers; but here all was visible which related to the 'poetry of motion'." In Cleveland, in the same state, some two hundred ladies had come out in the new style, whilst a hundred miles away at Toledo in the evening there had been held "a large and elegant party where nearly every lady present, some sixty or seventy, had the good taste to come out in the new costume".

At Battle Creek, Michigan, some thirty-one young women in "semi-oriental costume" had turned out in procession, and so had all the factory girls of Lowell, Massachusetts, who, as a result of their lady employer's exhortations and financial help, had also organized a Bloomer Institute that would meet on Wednesday evenings every week, for (1) Mutual Improvement in Literature, Science and Morals, (2) Emancipation from the thraldom of that dictatorial French goddess Fashion, and an exemplary enforcement of the Rights and Duty to dress according to the demands of Nature.

Under "Bloomerism in California" the *New York Tribune's* correspondent declared: "The most momentous topic which has excited the public mind for a long while is the new style of dress for ladies. One of our dressmakers placed a doll in her window equipped in the new style, and donned the like apparel while in her store. The newspapers got wind of the innovation and the editors all gave their opinions on the new costume, founded on personal observation. All day and in the evenings, a throng of men stood about the door and window to get a peep at the lady. Persons were hired to enter to make a purchase, so as to draw her from the back room into a position visible through the window. Men and women all over the city talked of nothing else. They scarcely dropped the subject an hour to discuss the hanging of the murderer, Stuart. The general impression is decidedly favourable, and I should not be surprised to see it generally adopted."

A similar attitude of approval was taken in early September by the *Advertiser* of Apalachicola, Florida, on the Gulf of Mexico when "on Thursday afternoon last our city was honoured by the appearance of three of Alabama's fairest daughters magnificently dressed in Bloomer Costume who, we understand, arrived here that morning in the schooner *Geneva* from a place of that name via Pensacola. Their sudden appearance produced quite a sensation among our quiet citizens; in fact we never saw a place more effectually stirred up. Most of the young men made their acquaintance immediately and some escorted them to all parts of the city, explaining the advantages and beauties of our metropolis as a summer residence.

"They were all dressed in most exquisite style, and we believe the new costume has met with the approval of most of our citizens. Miss Julia Mortimer, who attracted most of our attention, was richly dressed in a scarlet bodice and costly blue barège skirt, with fine white linen cambric pettiloons, tipped with lace and fastened around her small ankles with fancy ribands which gave her little feet an exquisite appearance.

"Miss Alice Gay displayed her charms with great effect; her complexion, a dark brunette, with her small piercing black eyes and raven tresses hanging loosely about her shoulders, made her almost irresistible. She wore a rich purple silk bodice and pink satin skirt; her short sleeves, fastened with diamond bracelets, gave her small hands that interest they so justly deserve.

"Miss Dorah De Kalb was dressed with the taste which quite showed her knowledge of that art to be superior to many of her sex; her blue scarf, scarlet bodice, and blue satin skirt admirably corresponded with her fair complexion; her swelling bosom which rose and fell as the perpetual motion of the sea, was adorned with a diamond breastpin, its brightness only equalled by her sparkling blue eyes.

"They all wore beautiful little gipsy hats, decorated with fresh rose-buds of every hue and colour. We had almost imagined when we first beheld them we were visited by a flock of fairy queens."

It pleased Amelia Bloomer to read such reports and to learn that the costume the world had named after her was making so many converts, despite all the ridicule. Gymnasts and skaters were now wearing it, and so were farmers' wives who found it ideal for heavy work. And it became the feminist battle dress—Lucy Stone, Lucretia Mott, Paulina Wright Davis, Theodosia Gilbert, Susan B. Anthony, Sarah Grimké and Angelina Grimké being amongst the most prominent.

When some elderly ladies wrote to Mrs. Bloomer to ask if she thought their wearing the costume would bring the feminist cause into disrepute, she answered: "Do just as your impulses move you to do. What you

Lucretia Mott.

Elizabeth Cady Stanton.

Bronze tablet commemorating the spot where the Wesleyan Chapel,
Seneca Falls, stood in which the first Women's Rights Convention in
the world's history was held on 19th and 20th July, 1848.

"Les Modes Parisiennes" for 1850.

IZOD'S PATENT CORSETS.

TRADE MARK. TRADE MARK.

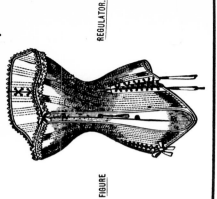

REGULATOR.

FIGURE

IZOD'S PATENT MOULDED TRADE MARK. SEWN CORSETS.

PEAR

BUSK

These Corsets may be had of all respectable Drapers and Ladies' Outfitters, at various prices, and in a variety of material, viz.:—White, Dove and Grey Coutille, Single or Double; White and Dove Satteen; also in Scarlet Lasting, and Black Italian Cloths.

They are made with either Plain or Pear-Shaped Busks.

The Belted Corset is also produced.

"The Steam-moulded Corsets of Messrs. IZOD and SON have obtained a justly-merited place in public estimation. These Corsets are composed of the best materials, are cut in exquisite proportion, are finished by steam-moulding, and are acknowledged model types of female form. Thus manufactured, it is by no means surprising that the feminine portion of the public inquire for these admirable Corsets of Draper and Milliner, and that the demand for these Corsets is increasing daily."—*The Milliner and Dressmaker.*

Upon the shape of the Corset entirely depends the accurate fit of a Lady's Dress or Costume.

The Patent Corsets of Messrs. IZOD and SON are cut in exquisite proportions, made of the best materials, and finished by their patent Steam-moulding Process, so that the fabric and bones are adapted with marvellous accuracy to every curve and undulation of the finest type of figure. These Corsets also give great support, and they fit so accurately and comfortably that a very small size can be worn without the slightest injury to the figure.

The variations in fashion are vigilantly watched,

"Lay figures or models have been constructed in

Victoria & Albert Museum.

Aids to wand-like waists.

THE LILY.

A MONTHLY JOURNAL, DEVOTED TO TEMPERANCE AND LITERATURE.

Published by a Committee of Ladies.—TERMS—Fifty Cents a Year, in Advance.

| VOL. 1. | SENECA FALLS, JANUARY 1, 1849. | NO. 1. |

POETRY.

[For Editors]—

The following lines are respectfully inscribed to
" The Lily," if you deem them a meet tracery for its
virgin leaves.

LINES.

" Drink stranger from this crystal cup!
Our Father placed it here,
Dew for the Lily's pearly lip,
And for the wanderer's cheer."

Thus stole a soft voice warblingly,
Like to a harp that is just set free ;
From a Lotus that hung by a fountain side,
As if it were the wavelet's bride.

A Youth was sitting with bended form,
'Mid the shadows of a wood ;
Where the plane tree lifted its gaudy grove,
And the pine its crested hood.

His eye was red, and his brain was hot,
For a fever had lurked there long;
Yet his face was pale as the cheek at night,
When Conscience bares its thong.

And he started when he heard that voice,
As from a dream's beguile ;
For it came like the chiding of one we love,
So sad, and yet a smile.

He looked around whence the voice might come,
But the guest and the chaunt were gone ;
Save the Lily that hung in the fountain's light,
Beautiful and alone.

He looked at the flower, and again he looked,
And yet he knew not why ;
For it minded him of a guileless heart,
And Purity's last sigh.

And in that little point of time,
On that still happy morn,
Years thrust their subtle panoply,
Of sorrow and of scorn.

Home ! forms that were ! the darkling tide
Deeper and wilder rushed ;
A boon that might have made him blest,
A boon that he had crushed.

And then that voice came startling near,
Solemn, the smile was cast,
And that low pleading came once more,
It was to be the last.

" Press not the wine-cup to thy palm,
Thou Wanderer ! again ;
Or it shall smite thee to thy soul,
With an undying pain.

Thy Mother's dying agony,

Thy Father's look of woe,
Alike are less a draught for thee,
Than thou again shalt know.

Hurl then the goblet from thy lip,
Thy parched lip, and see
That Heaven hath yet a gift of love,
Thou prayerless one, for thee !"

It ceased ! still motionless he bent
Beneath those shadows dim ;
Tears to another might have come,
They did not come to him.

Then he arose, and raised his hand,
As if grasping power not here ;
And uttered words that may not be
Uttered to mortal ear.

But one was there that heard that vow,
And sped unwearied flight ;
Nor paused till on Life's spotless page,
Was writ each word of light.

Twelve moons had waned, and hung their bows
Upon the eastern sky,
E'er 'mid those forest aisles again,
A youth trod pensively.

'Twas morn—and the red sun was not yet
On Elm and high Palm tree ;
Yet many a wing was glancing through
Their verdant balcony.

Yes—'twas the same, the very same—
The bank, the moss, the wood,
Where twelve swift passing months before,
An outcast wanderer stood.

And the fount was there and bathed the air,
With its misty veil of white ;
And still that " Lily" rose and laid
Its forehead to the light.

And the eye that looked upon the flower,
Was damp as its crystal cup ;
And with that twilight's morning star
One voice in praise went up.

Auburn, 1848.

SELECTED TALE.

THE OLD CLOAK.

BY MRS. D——.

" Pray, Mr. Norton," exclaimed a lively lady
to a fashionably dressed, handsome young man,
who was standing beside her at an evening party,
" pray, do you intend to remain an old Bachelor
all your days ! Since your return from Europe
I have been continually expecting to hear of your
marriage, but here you have been, two years, and
you are still, to all appearance, " in statu quo," as
the lawyers say."

" My dear Mrs. Hinton," replied the young
gentleman, with a smile, " I will be frank and tell
you the real reason of my remaining 'a general
admirer of the sex, instead of confining my attentions to any one ' bright, particular star,' however
much I may be dazzled by its brilliancy. I am
actually afraid to marry."

" Afraid !" echoed the lady, opening her dark
eyes to their widest extent with astonishment.—
" 'Faint heart never won,' you know. Are you
afraid to propose ?"

" No, madam, afraid to marry. You will laugh
at me, I dare say, when I tell you that my seat in
church has a great deal to do with my solitary
state, which seems so much to excite your surprise."

" Why, yes," replied Mrs. Hinton, " one is
always surprised when a young man who—without meaning to flatter you—is certainly a favorite
in society, (here Mr. Norton made her a polite
bow,) and who has an independent fortune, still
refrains from choosing one of the many fair damsels whom he meets, to superintend his establishment. But what influence your seat in church
can have upon the matter I am at a loss to ima-
gine."

" You must know, then, that I sit just behind
Miss La Mode, in Dr. Rightbead's church, and
the sight of her velvet cloak absolutely frightens
me from the thought of marrying, a wife who
may some day say to me, ' My dear, I am dying
for a new velvet cloak ; please to give me two or
three hundred dollars, and I will go to Stewart's
and buy one.' How I should shudder to hear
such a request."

" Really, Mr. Norton, this is too absurd, for
you, with your fortune, to talk in such a manner.
I shall begin to think you a miser. Your wife
might dress as extravagantly as she chose, and it
would not injure you. And surely you do not
object to a lady's wearing a velvet cloak !"

" I do not object to anything that is consistent
but I cannot help thinking splendid velvet, such
as Queen Victoria herself might be satisfied with
for a coronation robe, sadly out of place when it
is made into a cloak, to be worn on almost all occasions ; particularly when it is well known that
Miss La Mode's father does not even pay his ba-
ker or his butcher. If I were one of his poor
creditors I should be tempted to take back the
mantle from the young lady, in the street, and sell it for
what it would bring."

Mrs. Hinton sat silent at this speech. Her
conscience reproached her, for she knew that she
had, on that day, purchased an elegant new mantle, although her husband had requested her to be
as economical as possible in her expenditures, as
he found it difficult, in those trying times, to meet
all the demands made upon his purse. She was
a woman whose warmth of generous feelings, as yet un-
hardened by resisting good impulses, and she se-
cretly resolved to take back the mantle the next
day and prevail upon the shop-man to receive it,
since it was not yet paid for. All this passed
through her mind with the rapidity of lightning.

The front page of the first issue of *The Lily*.

The Bloomer Costume—lithograph by N. Currier.

Fashions for 1851. Bloomerism, a new costume for ladies.

"The Band at St. James's Palace." Cartoon by J. Leech from *Punch* of 1851.

EFFICIENCY OF THE POLICE IN WHAT IS VULGARLY CALLED A "JOLLY ROW."

Cartoon by J. Leech from *Punch* of 1851.

"A Quiet Smoke." Cartoon by J. Leech from *Punch* of 1851.

"Shopping." Cartoon by J. Leech from *Punch* of 1851.

POPPING THE QUESTION.

Superior Creature. "SAY! OH, SAY DEAREST! WILL YOU BE MINE?" &C., &C.

Cartoon by J. Leech from *Punch* of 1851.

Cover of Music Sheet 1851. Erroneously inscribed to Mrs. Colonel
Bloomer instead of Mrs. Dexter C. Bloomer.

BLOOMERISM

OR, THE

FOLLIES of the DAY

With New Scenery, Dresses, & Appointments.

AND AS AN OVERTURE,

The New Adelphi Bloomer Polka,

COMPOSED BY ALFRED MELLON.

☞ *Extract from the Kirk Session Register of Perth, showing the consequence in former times of putting on the Breeks.*---

"April 16, 1632. Conform to citation, compeared Jane Gibson, a servant lass, and is accused of indecent wantonness in putting on men's clothes upon her. She answered that she simply drew upon her a pair of breeks, and cast them off immediately, and she promised never to do the like hereafter. She is committed to ward, therein to remain the space of three hours."

QUIS REBUS *DEXTER* MODUS.---*Virgil.*

Mr. Agricola Green,	{ a retired Tailor, fond of novelties, a conscientious cabbagerian, much given to Vegetables and Quietness }	Mr. G. HONEY,
Mr. Flighty Bounce,	{ a man and a brother, fond of everything but his business, a great advocate of universal peace, except in his own house }	Mr. PAUL BEDFORD,
Mr. Jenkinson,	(a "Representative of the Press" with a great swallow for news and eatables)	Mr. S. EMERY,
r. Slowman,	(a true Briton, devoted to the good old times and home productions)	Mr. WOOLGAR,
Mr. Weakly,	(a Teatotaler and Hydropathist)	Mr. WORRELL,
Count Knoweroff,	(one of the Foreign Contributions to the Great Exhibition not in the Catalogue)	Mr. C. J. SMITH,
Mr. Muddles,	(a believer in Mesmerism, the Phonetic Noos, and O.D.V.	Mr. CULLENFORD,
John Airey,	(a Policeman, much given to sofs wittles and hard swearing)	Mr. O. SMITH,
Newsboy,	Mr. WOODWARD,	
Mrs. Portia Lucretia Green,	{ a strong minded woman, and a determined advocate of the rights of Women and Bloomerism }	Miss WOOLGAR,
Mrs. Bounce,	(with an Air) Miss KATHLEEN FITZWILLIAM,	
Mrs. Muddles,	Mrs. LAWS,	Mrs. Slowman, Mrs. WOOLLIDGE,
	Mrs. Weakly, Miss TAYLOR,	

Sairey Potts, (Maid of all work, & a little Play—a hater of all new fangled notions except Policemen) Miss E. CHAPLIN.

Bloomer Friends, By Messrs. RIDGEWAY, LINDON, FREEBORN, COX, BUTLER, MITCHENSON. Mesdames LELACHEUR, HEALEY, TOMPSON, ROBINS, McCLEWEE, LOUISE, MITCHENSON, &c.

IN THE COURSE OF THE PIECE,

A GRAND

VEGETARIAN BANQUET

AND

A Lecture on Bloomerism!

RESULTING IN THE

BLOOMER POLKA!

With Twelve Pretty Bloomers all in a row.

Victoria & Albert Museum.

Adelphi Theatre poster, 1851, from the Enthoven Collection.

Miss Woolgar as Mrs. Portia Lucretia Green in "Bloomerism—or The Follies
of the Day." Adelphi Theatre, October 1851.

find a burden in belief or apparel cast off. You old women of sixty have been slaves to the tyrant long enough, and, as you have but a few years remaining to live, be as free and as happy as you can what time remains. Fit yourselves for a higher sphere, and cease grovelling in the dirt. Let there be no stain of earth upon your soul or apparel."

Although Mrs. Bloomer encouraged the wearing of the costume by young and old, she had secret qualms. She suddenly found herself to be known all over the world as its sponsor, and more and more people took out subscriptions to *The Lily* every day. She was even offered a high fee to go on a lecture tour of England. A modern work on the period alleges that she went, but this is incorrect. She never left America.

Such fame meant that she found herself in a position from which she could not retreat even if she had so desired. She therefore told everybody that she found the costume comfortable, light, easy and convenient, and continued to wear it on all occasions, at home and on journeys, at church and on the lecture platform, at fashionable parties and in the Post Office. She stubbornly made up her mind that she would go on wearing it until the papers ceased making fun of her.

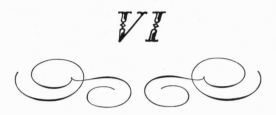

VI

THE WORLD LAUGHS

THE FIRST comment in English newspapers on the Bloomer Costume appeared in *The Times* for Thursday, May 31st, 1851. This under the heading, "A Lady Resolved To Be Free and Easy", limited itself to quoting from what Amelia had written in the May issue of *The Lily*.

Some weeks later, the *Illustrated London News* appeared on July 19th with a picture of Mrs. Bloomer in the new attire, and an article headed: "The American Ladies' New Costume". This stated that a decided novelty in female attire was just then absorbing much of the attention of the ladies of the northern states of New York.

It was not long before Englishwomen were experimenting with the costume. An "Association of Bloomers" was formed by those in favour of it. *The Times* for Monday, September 15th, tells of "Bloomerism in Piccadilly". It reported how on the preceding Friday forenoon two young ladies with two companions who might have been their mothers alighted from a cab "in the peculiar dress so often described of late, and proceeding towards the entrance to the Green Park, distributed in their way handbills containing a spirited appeal to the women of England to throw off the yoke of their unfeeling and brutal oppressors, and adopt an attire better suited to the dignity of the equal of man. In a short time, the pressure of the crowd became so great that the missionaries found it convenient to call a cab, which they entered amid much laughter, mingled with cheering."

Then on Saturday, September 27th, *The Times* drew its readers' attentions to "Bloomerism at the Crystal Palace". On the Thursday afternoon of that same week, visitors to the Great Exhibition in Hyde Park were startled to see three ladies dressed in the new style and accompanied by "gentlemen wearing the habiliments of the new sect" appear in the large open space to the west of the Crystal Palace. They seemed to be "persons of some station in Society, and bore with considerable good humour the taunts which were freely directed against them. They walked round the building, followed by a large number of persons, who had been attracted towards them by the novelty of their dress, but did not enter the Exhibition.

"They carried with them a quantity of printed bills, announcing a lecture by one of their order in Finsbury on Monday evening next, and these they politely distributed among such persons as were willing to accept them. After remaining on the ground about an hour and a half, they rode away in a phaeton which was waiting for them. It was stated that two of the ladies belonged to a family of great respectability residing in Torrington Square."

These bills were widely circulated throughout London, and as the result on Monday, September 29th, an immense number of people assembled at the Royal British Institution, City Road, to hear the advertised lecture by the "apostle of Bloomerism" as the wags called her, Mrs. C. H. Dexter from America.

Every door of the building was besieged and stormed by the crowds. An eye-witness states that by eight o'clock every nook and corner of the large school-room was completely filled, the ledges of the wall, and even the rafters being turned into perches by some adventurous spirits. When this inflowing had been accomplished to the full capacity of the building, those within set their backs against the doors and successfully resisted the further influx of the sightseeing mob, of whom the greater part were men.

Half past eight arrived, but no Mrs. Dexter. Those who had paid their money naturally waxed impatient and began to indulge themselves "in fun, noises and other popular amusements so thoroughly congenial to the tastes of a large set of enlightened waiting Englishmen". But time wore on, and at last a member of the "London Bloomer Committee" announced from the platform that Mrs. Dexter would appear as soon as the audience conducted themselves properly. This, perhaps, was not the most judicious way of securing silence.

"Then Mr. Dexter appeared in the nondescript dress of his order, and said that his lady would appear as soon as the police could clear a way for her outside, and a few minutes afterwards announced that she was in the building and only waited till order could be commanded to come forward. This alternate speechifying of Mr. Dexter and the committee-man continued till nearly ten o'clock, not one word out of a dozen being heard on account of the cries for order and facetious observations of the visitors."

At last, a young lady on the platform grew so im-

68

patient that she shouted at Mr. Dexter that the whole thing was a hoax and defied him to produce his wife. He promised that he would and went in search of her, but did not return. Ten minutes later an usher brought the news that both Mr. and Mrs. Dexter had left the building and that the lecture had been postponed until the following Monday.

The frustrated audience started yelling for the return of their entrance money (3d.) but the usher said they would have to discuss that with Mr. Dexter. It was well past ten o'clock before they were persuaded to disperse.

The postponed lecture was held in Miss Kelly's Theatre in Dean Street, Soho. A crowd assembled in the street long before the doors were opened, and when admission was obtained the theatre was immediately filled —so rapidly, indeed, that a gentleman from the stage announced that the lecture would not be delayed until the time named on the bills as the edifice could contain no more.

A few minutes after this, about twenty ladies in the Bloomer Costume appeared upon the boards and took their seats in a semi-circle. Every variety of the new dress was now to be seen, from the strictly legitimate Bloomer skirt, "two inches below the knee", to the less daring and less attractive drapery which came down almost to the ankles. Nor were varieties of colour wanting. Young ladies in white with pink sashes contrasted strangely with elderly ladies in brown and black, some preferring the hair unadorned, others displaying a few ornaments, and two wearing huge broad-brimmed hats.

"The audience, mostly of men, received the Bloomer cortège with cheers and laughter, causing some of the ladies to waver in their approach, and two retired behind the slips to regain their presence of mind,

69

somewhat shaken by their reception." Thus ran the report in *The Times* next day.

Order having been restored, Mrs. Dexter, dressed in a dark brown costume, gave her lecture in which she attacked the then style of women's dress and urged all ladies to follow Mrs. Bloomer's example. Her evident sincerity made some impression and on the whole the address was favourably received. The Bloomer ladies then joined in the National Anthem at the close of the proceedings.

A further lecture was given on the Tuesday evening, enlivened by a parade of living models wearing present and past fashions. Referring to the baneful effect of the compression of the waist, Mrs. Dexter asked how could they expect the heart or lungs to perform their proper functions when they only allotted to them half the space provided by the Creator?

On Wednesday evening yet another lecture was delivered in Miss Kelly's Theatre, but this was not so well patronized as the admission charge had been raised from threepence to one shilling.

The final lecture of the series took place on the Saturday evening. The audience was in jovial mood and laughed at everything, even when Mrs. Dexter related what was intended to be a heartbreaking story. She ended by saying that Mrs. Bloomer's name would be handed down to posterity with greater glory than those of their most distinguished generals. She deserved far more praise than the Duke of Wellington himself.

"At the close," wrote *The Times* reporter, "she was recalled by unanimous acclamation to receive a more stunning, deafening round of applause than had been indulged in during the lecture."

The same issue of *The Times* revealed that the great reformer, Lord Shaftesbury, whom one might have expected to support Bloomerism, actually disapproved of it. When addressing Mrs. Chisholm's group meeting of intending colonists, he warned female emigrants not to import such attire into the countries they intended to colonize.

The Costume was a godsend to the theatre, and no fewer than three farces on the theme were produced in London that autumn, all with great success.

At "Punch's Playhouse and Strand Theatre" on Monday, September 15th, was presented a triple bill which opened with the 37th performance of "The Shot Tower, a Dramatic Bubble"; the first performance of "A Hopeless Passion, a Petite Comedy"; and the first performance also of "A Figure of Fun, or the Bloomer Costume". The last was praised next day by the critic of *The Theatrical Journal* as "one of the best pieces of the kind which has been produced for a long time; it is acted very cleverly".

Within three weeks a rival farce had opened at the Adelphi Theatre, which was managed by the astute Mr. Benjamin Webster. The triple bill for Thursday, October 2nd, included the one act Comic Opera, "Good Night, Signor Pantalon!"; the Comic Drama, "The Forest Rose and the Yankee Plough Boy"; and "Bloomerism, or the Follies of the Day", which was billed as "an entirely laughable *Pièce de Circonstance*, with New Scenery, Dresses, and Appointments". It had for overture "The New Adelphi Bloomer Polka", composed by Alfred Mellon. The star was Miss Woolgar in the part of Mrs. Portia Lucrece Green, a strong-minded woman and a determined advocate of the rights of Women and Bloomerism.

The play bill advertising this farce announced that in the course of the piece there would be "A Grand Vegetarian Banquet, and a Lecture on Bloomerism—

71

resulting in the Bloomer Polka with Twelve Pretty Bloomers all in a row!"

On Friday, November 14th, at the Olympic Theatre, Strand, the theatrical fare consisted of "The Annals of the French Revolution" and for the first time "The Original Bloomers".

In the provinces, too, the public flocked to see these plays produced in their local theatres. Even as far north as Aberdeen, the Scots enjoyed "Bloomerism" when produced at the Theatre Royal.

In October, the following advertisement appeared in London papers: "BLOOMER COSTUME. Five beautiful varieties, by which the public may judge if this dress may ever become popular, are now added to MADAME TUSSAUD AND SON'S EXHIBITION. Admission to LARGE ROOM AND HALL of KINGS, 1S. NAPOLEON'S SHRINE and CHAMBER OF HORRORS, 6d. Open from 11 till dusk. BAZAAR, BAKER-ST., PORTMAN-SQUARE."

This proved a tremendous attraction, and soon an extra "Bloomer" was added. In the *Theatrical Journal* for November 26th, a writer describes a visit to the Exhibition. "It is always with great pleasure we visit this place, where there is so much to feast the eye and instruct the mind. In our perambulations, we arrived at a most pleasing group; here we beheld six beautiful female figures dressed most elegantly in the new Bloomer Costume. This group attacts the company to a great extent, and no wonder, for the whole of them are different in feature and expression of countenance; the dresses are both costly and elegant, and do infinite credit to those who have had the arrangement of the group."

The fact that three theatres were presenting Bloomer farces to packed audiences made Mr. Benjamin Webster shrewdly decide to dress all the ladies in his annual pantomime in the Bloomer Costume. So he announced as his "Great Attraction for the Christmas Holidays" at the Theatre Royal, Haymarket, opening on Boxing Night "an entirely New Romantic Fairy Extravaganza (in Two Acts) called 'The Princess Radiant—or Mayflower'."

Loud applause greeted Mrs. L. S. Buckingham when on the first night she made an imposing entreé as Princess Radiant at the head of her troupe of Amazons singing: "I Want To Be A Bloomer". Then according to the playbill, she made a "Successful Assertion of the Rights of Women".

Even Paris presented a Bloomer play. *Bentley's Miscellany* contains this report from that city: "There is a clever little Vaudeville now performing here, entitled '1851 et 1951', where a fair Bloomer (no longer in the bud, but full-blown) accosts a military specimen of the weaker (?) sex in the street, and is remonstrated with by the gallant warrior in the words, '*Ah! Mademoiselle, vous allez me compromettre!*' "

The Bloomer farces of 1851 have long since been forgotten. Of more lasting value, perhaps were the Staffordshire China Figures, about nine inches high, supposed to represent Mrs. Bloomer, which were made that year and are now collectors' rarities. One figure shows a woman in a broad-brimmed and plumed hat, worn on the back of her head and an umbrella in her left hand, whilst a more masculine version is of a woman wearing a man's collar and bow tie and holding a cigar instead of an umbrella.

For months, *Punch* writers and artists made the Bloomer and its wearers their butt. Women of all shapes and sizes were depicted in the cartoons of Leech, wearing Bloomers and being watched by gaping men and

73

cheeky urchins, making such remarks as—"Oh, what rummy trotters!" or "She's queerish about the hocks!" or "She's a good plucked 'un!"

Punch published a mock message from Mrs. Bloomer in which she exhorted every British bride to be married in a Bloomer. No woman must consent to take a husband who, at the last minute, will not take his wife full blooming—and, of course, the bridesmaids must be dressed in the new style.

It is a fickle world. Turning back the pages of *Punch*, one finds that only the previous year those who pilloried the Bloomer had been pillorying the Petticoat: "We know of none, among numerous acts of utility performed by ladies in the present day, involving so much self-sacrifice as the practice adopted by our fashionably dressed women of cleaning the public thoroughfares. Few who have not watched the elegantly habited female pedestrians passing through thick and thin can form any idea of what she carries in her train, when she sets the example we have alluded to."

In the fastness of their clubs, the gentlemen of England chortled over *Punch*, whilst in the music halls and taverns, the Cider Cellars, the Coal Holes, and the Holes in the Wall, the lower orders laughed at songs and jokes about the Bloomer. A popular broadsheet of 1851, "I'll be a Bloomer", went:

> "Listen, females all
> No matter what your trade is,
> Old Nick is in the girls,
> The Devil's in the ladies!
> Married men may weep,
> And tumble in the ditches,
> Since women are resolved
> To wear the shirts and breeches.

Ladies do declare
A change should have been sooner,
The women, one and all,
Are going to join the Bloomers.
Prince Albert and the Queen
Had such a jolly row, sirs;
She threw off stays and put
On waistcoat, coat, and trousers.

The world's turned upside down;
The ladies will be tailors,
And serve Old England's Queen
As soldiers and as sailors.
Won't they look funny when
The seas are getting lumpy,
Or when they ride astride
Upon an Irish donkey?..."

In the ballrooms they danced to rival versions of the "Bloomer Waltz", the "Bloomer Schottische", the "Bloomer Quadrille", and the "Bloomer Polka"—composed by Mr. J. J. Blockley or Mr. W. H. Montgomery or Mr. Alfred Mellon. There was also yet another "Bloomer Polka" by "Carlotta". This claimed to be the Original Bloomer Polka.

Excitement about the fashion reached its peak in London when some bright young sparks formed a committee and organized a Bloomer Ball, to which only ladies dressed in the Bloomer Costume would be admitted. There was much speculation as to who would attend. High-spirited girls asked one another, "Are you going, Maria? Will your Mamma let you? If she chaperones, will she, too, have to wear Bloomers?"

On the day of the Ball, crowds gathered early in Hanover Square, all determined to watch the arrival

75

of the Bloomer-clad beauties and their escorts at the Hanover Street Assembly Rooms. Some came to cheer, and others to boo. Hucksters and buskers plied a busy trade. One adventurous sailor boy on leave tied his bell-bottomed trousers round his ankles with string, borrowed a shawl and draped it about his middle to resemble a short skirt. Then he climbed up on to a balcony, and in a high falsetto recited the mock "Bloomerite Marching Song" to the delight of the waiting throng.

"Now then, my dear,
We'll smoke and cheer and drink our lager beer.
We'll have our latch-keys, stay out late at nights,
And boldly we'll assert our Female Rights,
While conquered men, our erstwhile tyrant foes
Shall stay at home and wear our cast-off clothes,
Nurse babies, scold the servants, get our dinners;
'Tis all that they are fit for, the wretched sinners!"

As the hour drew near, the "Peelers" were forced to clear a way for the carriages, and when the first equipage came spanking up, drawn by a pair of high-stepping greys with harness jingling, an expectant hush fell on the spectators. Papas hoisted their children on to their shoulders. Others hurriedly climbed lamp posts and the railings, so as to get a better view. Then there came groans of disappointment—for no Bloomer Beauties emerged out of the carriage, but only two elderly whiskered rakes, who winked knowingly at the crowd before disappearing through the portals.

Now carriage after carriage, cab after cab, arrived and disgorged its contents beneath the awning, while in the Assembly Rooms themselves, the orchestras tuned up in the gallery and the waiters manned the laden buffets beneath it. The bucks lounged about gracefully, watching the new arrivals, but nobody danced. Let *Punch* reveal the reason why:

"Gents—produce your fifteen shillings, take a cab and pay the fare.

Bid the driver wait till wanted, near to Hanover's famed Square.

'Tis the place, and all around it crowds collect to shout and call

At the people driving onward to attend the Bloomer Ball.

Bloomer Ball—that in the papers promised much that might attract

Quite an overflow of people, rushing like a cataract.

Oh, oh, my Bloomers, chicken-hearted! Oh, my Bloomers, what a fall!

Oh, the dreary, dreary aspect of the barren Bloomer Ball!

Seedier than fancy dresses, dirtier than showman's stocks,

Half-a-dozen pairs of trousers, half-a-dozen school-girls' frocks.

'Tis as well, perchance the ladies should avoid the London dirt

By a higher range of clothing and a somewhat shorter skirt.

But it cannot be expected we shall ever see the day

When, in gentlemanly trousers, they'll be figuring away,

As the husband, shall the wife be. He will have to wear a gown

If he does not quickly make her put her Bloomer shortcoat down.

'Tis the Ball—but, oh, how dreary! Men and women don't combine;

77

For, the latter to the former, are as one to ninety-
nine.
Thinly scattered are the females, scorning custom's
decent rules.
Dense the many men assembled, looking like a pack
of fools. . . .
But the crowd was disappointed, seeing what it witnessed then;
Scarcely half-a-dozen Bloomers, nearly seven hundred men."

But perhaps *Punch* was exaggerating for satire's sake.
The Times reported that between thirty and forty ladies
were there, though its correspondent suspected that they
had adopted the dress for the night only "as they would
have put on a masquerade costume for Vauxhall, which,
perhaps, would have been their more fitting arena". He
goes on to report that many variations of the costume
were worn, objecting very strongly to those ladies who
were crowned by large straw hats "the size of a small
table". Such head-dress was inappropriate for a ballroom. Nevertheless, he grudgingly admitted that there
were some "who were really dressed very nicely, their
clothes fitted beautifully, and ladies may depend that as
much art is required in cutting out the 'Bloomers' as
in masculine trousers, and that till experienced milliners
take the affair in hand, the converts to the new dress
will never look presentable".

The correspondent also noted that among the hundreds of men present were "most of the officers of the
'Guards' now in town". From the gallery, between the
dances, the large concert room appeared filled by a
dense mass of men through which here and there might
be discerned something surmounted with a nodding
plume where a "Bloomer" was trying to get through the

crowd. "During the dances, the lookers-on formed a ring four or five deep, or stood upon the benches round the room, contracting the space for the dancers to the narrowest possible limits, and threatening to take away that little, till one or two couples more adventurous than the rest dashed through the ring like a steamer charging a field of ice, and made an opening."

The report ends with several strictures. "It would be unfair to saddle the 'Bloomers' with all the sins committed at their ball, but there is one thing they do not do—they do not observe the old proverb: 'Practise what you preach.' Having attended many of their lectures, we can most unhesitatingly state that the polka was denounced in the most emphatic terms as an indelicate and improper dance. It was brought in as an instance of one of the immodest things the fashionable world tolerated, although the same fashion forbade them to shorten their petticoats. After having been set down in this style, who would expect to see the polka at a 'Bloomer Ball'? Every accession to the fair sex, when there were so few, was of great value, but that is no reason why they should have been cheered and crowded round on their entrance to the hindrance of the dancing, or anything else. Supper may be a very exhilarating thing, but that does not excuse a battle royal in the supper room with pieces of bread and orange and jelly."

The furore over the costume was not limited to London. At the end of August that year, the *Caledonian Mercury* bore the heading: "Bloomerism in Edinburgh". The report went: "Considerable surprise and amusement was occasioned on Thursday night by the appearance on the Dean-bridge of two ladies—one about 40 and another about 15 years her junior, wearing the Bloomer garb in its fullest style. The elderly lady was dressed in a long ruby coloured silk mantle, or polka, which partially hid that portion of the dress in which the aggression is most daringly manifested. Over the upper garment there seemed to be something like a shorter one of the same shape, bound round the waist with a rich shawl. The 'continuations' were nearly of the same colour, and reached to the instep of the foot. The young lady's dress was exactly similar in shape, but considerably lighter in colour. The bonnet in the case of the one was plain, like that of more decorous ladies, while the other wore a straw one, somewhat of a gypsy shape. The singular spectacle thus presented attracted considerable attention, even in the retired quarter of the town where it was witnessed, and comments character-ized by freedom more than politeness were now and again made by urchins who followed the unblushing Bloomers. From inquiries afterwards made, we learn that the ladies are Americans; but whether the new costume was assumed on this occasion by way of trial, or as a regular street dress, we have been unable to find out."

In the middle of October there came a newspaper report of "Bloomerism in Arbroath". "A considerable sensation was created in our market place on Saturday by the appearance of a lady—young, beautiful and aristocratic—on a fiery steed, habited à la Bloomer. She wore a hat, habit and trousers. The material of the latter was of substantial cloth, of a darkish hue, with the ex-tremities tightly strapped below the boot. The equip-ment was most becoming, and certainly an improvement on horsemanship worthy of imitation."

Mrs. Fanny Kemble, who claimed to have worn the Costume before America thought of it, met with dis-aster when she went out riding in it on the Grand Parade at Brighton towards the end of October. She was thrown from her horse with great violence and narrowly escaped serious injury. She was taken to her hotel, but after a few hours she rallied, and gave the readings which had already been announced for that evening at the Newburgh Rooms, "where she met with a hearty reception from a crowded audience, several of whom evinced great anxiety as to her safety".

In *The Month—A View of Passing Subjects and Manners* edited and mostly written and illustrated by Albert Smith and John Leech, appeared the following parody:

"Trousers or no trousers—that is the question;
Whether it is better on the legs to suffer
The dirt and scrapings of the bespatter'd crossings,
Or to take arms against the present Fashion,
And with new dresses change it?—to fix, to change,
No more; and by this change to say we stop
Mud splashing, and the thousand natural woes
The legs are heir to, 'tis an emendation
Devoutly to be wished. To fix, to change,
To change again! Perchance the gown; aye, there's
  the rub;
For in that change of dress what jeers may come
When we have shuffled off this flouncéd coil,
Must we then pause? Where's the respect
That makes the petticoats for so long rife?
For who would bear the great constraint of gowns,
The dresses long, the small feet hid thereby,
The pangs of tight-laced stays, the waist's display,
The dirtiness of stockings, and the turns
The patient follower of fashion takes
When she herself might her own comfort make
With pairs of trousers?"

But despite all Mrs. Dexter's lectures and the

crusading zeal of her supporters, British women as a whole were not yet ready for such a radical dress reform. Commenting on this "attempted revolution in female dress", the *Annual Register* for 1851 tells us that "a few dashing damsels—of what character is unknown —sported the hybrid garments in some public places; but the dress, having been adopted by women whose character was not at all doubtful, and by barmaids of public houses, the absurdity died away."

Although this version of the Bloomer Costume had but a short life in England, it lasted longer in the country of its birth and played an important part in furthering the Women's Rights Movement.

Let the final comment come from the *New York Journal*: "If ever a lady waked up one morning and found herself famous, that woman was Mrs. Bloomer; she has immortalized her name, and the Bloomer Costume will become as celebrated as Mary Queen of Scots' Cap, the Elizabeth Ruff, or the Pompadour Robe."

VII

MOSES FORBIDS IT

IN THE spring of 1852, a Women's Temperance
Society covering the whole of the State of New York
came into being, following a meeting of some en-
thusiastic "Daughters of Temperance" at Rochester.
Elizabeth Cady Stanton was elected President, Mrs.
Bloomer Corresponding Secretary, and two school-
teachers, Miss Susan B. Anthony and Mrs. Mary C.
Vaughan, Recording Secretaries.

At this gathering, a resolution was proposed that "no
woman should remain in the relation of wife to the confirmed drunkard" and that drunkenness should become
legal grounds for divorce. It was in favour of this that
Amelia made her maiden speech, and received an ova-
tion when she sat down. They now knew that the
Editress of *The Lily* could use her tongue as eloquently
as she could her pen. Needless to say, the resolution was
carried.

In the autumn of the same year, the men's State
Temperance Society held its annual convention at Syracuse. All other temperance organizations were invited

to send delegates. Mrs. Bloomer and Miss Anthony were chosen by the women's society as its representatives and attended. Their arrival in the town caused a stir, as they were both dressed in the Bloomer Costume.

A resident of the town, Mrs. Russell Sage, recorded this description of Mrs. Bloomer in her Memoirs: "Her manner was unpretentious, quiet and delicately feminine. Her costume showed a total disregard for effect, and was mannish only to the extent of practicability. Her bodice was soft and belted at the waist, her collar simple and correct, as was also her prim bonnet. Her skirt fell half way from knee to ankle, beneath which she wore her bloomers—really pantalets—made of black material as the rest of her costume, and reaching to her boot tops. She is entirely what she claims to be—a practical woman, progressive and competent of realizing results from her theories."

The two delegates arrived in Syracuse the evening before the convention was due to open. Next morning, just as they were preparing to go to the hall, they were told that a gentleman wished to see them in the hotel parlour. They found Samuel J. May, a prominent member of the men's society, awaiting them. He revealed that their arrival had upset some of the clergymen attending the convention who, shocked at the idea of women delegates, had threatened to withdraw if they were admitted.

This threat had alarmed others who were not quite so conservative, but who did not want to incur the risk of a disturbance in the hall. They had therefore persuaded Mr. May to wait upon the two ladies and to urge them to leave the town.

Mr. May was very diplomatic, merely stating the facts, and allowing Mrs. Bloomer and Miss Anthony to make their own decision without any pressure either way from him. But when they decided to go to the hall and present their credentials and demand their rights as members invited to the convention, his face beamed with joy. "You are right to go," he said.

Mrs. Bloomer described what happened in *The Lily* when, at the appointed time, the two women took their seats at the side of the platform. "The Rev. Dr. Mandeville of Albany rose, turned his chair facing us, his back to the audience, and stared at us with all the impudence of a boor, as if to wither us with his piercing glance. Mr. William A. Burleigh then read the Annual Report, which among other things hailed the formation of the Women's State Society as a valuable auxiliary in the cause of temperance. The Rev. J. Marsh moved that the report be accepted and adopted."

The Lily then goes on to say that Dr. Mandeville objected in a speech of some length "characterized by more venom and vulgarity than it had ever before been our fortune to hear; and such as the most foul-mouthed politician or bar-room orator would have hesitated to utter before respectable audiences. He denounced the Women's State Temperance Society. He called the women who belonged 'a hybrid species, half man and half woman, belonging to neither sex'. This Society and the Women's Rights Movement must be put down, cut up root and branch."

Dr. Mandeville wound up with a threat that if the report was adopted without striking out the offending sentence, he would dissolve his connection with the Society. Having thus discharged his venom and issued his commands, he took his hat, left the hall with a pompous air and did not again show himself at the convention.

Pandemonium followed. "We had friends who were as determined on their side that women should be

85

recognized. A dozen men talked at the same time, all over the floor, each insisting on being heard—till all became confusion, a babel of voices. No order could be kept, and the President left his chair in disgust. Time and words fail to give you the details of this disgraceful meeting. The ringleaders were prominent clergymen of Albany, Lockport, and Buffalo."

Mrs. Bloomer then tells her readers that the names and faces of these men who made many insulting remarks about her costume were indelibly engraven on her memory. "During this whole day's quarrel of the men, no woman said a word except once. Miss Anthony addressed the chair, intending to prefer a request for a donation of temperance tracts for distribution by our society. She got no further than 'Mr. President' when she was rudely called to order by one of the belligerent clergymen and told to sit down."

With great dignity, Miss Anthony sat down among rival cries of "Hear the lady! Let her speak! Go on, go on!" and "Never—never! Order! Don't let her, Mr. President!"

The President was asked to give a decision. He ruled that the constitution of the Society and also the invitations sent out for the meeting, would admit women to an equal participation in the proceedings, and allow her a vote; but as there were no female societies in existence five years previously when the society was organized, such a thing was not contemplated at that time. He therefore considered women inadmissible. "The letter of the constitution and the call would admit her, but the spirit would not."

The President's ruling was challenged, and after a furious debate it was put to the vote. The majority in favour was only two. *The Lily* summed up: "And so, after spending the whole afternoon in hot discussion of the women's rights question, the disgraceful affair terminated by refusing woman the right of uttering her sentiments on a subject in which she was deeply interested."

Not all the Cloth, however, were in the opposite camp. A local clergyman, the Rev. Luther Lee, offered his church just before the adjournment of the convention that stormy day, and Mr. May announced that Mrs. Bloomer and Miss Anthony would speak there in the evening. They had a crowded house, whilst the anti-feminists in the other hall scarcely numbered fifty.

"The same battle," wrote Mrs. Bloomer later, "was fought over and over again in various parts of New York State, and the most deadly opposition came from the clergy, though a few noble men in that profession ever remained true through all the conflicts of those days."

The newspapers, too, could be very hostile. A report in the *Star* of Syracuse reads: "The women at the Tomfoolery Convention being held in this city are brawling creatures, supported by Aunt Nancy men, Abolitionists of the most frantic and contemptible kind, Women's Righters and preachers of such damnable doctrines and accursed heresies as would make demons of the pit shudder to hear. We have selected a few appropriate passages from God's Bible for the consideration of the infuriated gang (Bloomers and all) at the Convention: Gen. iii. 16; Tit. ii. 4, 5; Prov. ix. 13, xxi. 9, 19; 1 Cor. xi. 8, 9; 1 Tim. ii. 8-14; 1 Cor. xiv. 34, 35; Eph. v. 22-24."

One minister in Syracuse preached a sermon against them and had it printed in pamphlet form. These he sent out by hundreds to other ministers of his church throughout the state for them to distribute among the women of their congregation, with the intention of "heading off this new movement of women". In this sermon, the Rev. D. Talmage quoted Moses as an authority for women not wearing men's attire, and forbade any female members of his flock to wear the Bloomer Costume.

In the next issue of *The Lily* Amelia hit back, pointing out that there were laws of fashion in dress older than Moses, and that the first one mentioned in the Bible was that set by Adam and Eve, when they sewed fig-leaves together and made themselves aprons. She could find nothing in the Book of Genesis to suggest that his apron was bifurcated and hers was not—that hers was long and his was short. The obvious assumption was that they were dressed alike.

"The second fashion was made by God himself, and it would be supposed that if He intended the sexes to be distinguished by their garments, explicit directions would have been given as to the style of each. 'Unto Adam, also, and unto his wife, did the Lord God make coats of skins and clothed them.'—Genesis iii. 21."

Not a word as to any difference in the cut and make-up of the coat, Mrs. Bloomer stressed. No command to Eve that she must "swathe and cripple herself in long, tight, heavy, draggling skirts, while Adam dons the more comfortable, healthy bifurcated garment. God clothed them just alike, and made no signs that henceforth they should be distinguished by their apparel. And for long years, there was little, if any, difference."

After describing the dress of different ancient nations, Egyptians, Babylonians, Israelites, Persians, Romans, Saxons, Normans, Turks, and Chinese, and demonstrating that there was no essential difference between the garb worn by men and women, Amelia proceeds: "With all the history of male and female attire before him, and with so much proof of the similarity in dress, how can Mr. Talmage set up the claim that men have a right to any particular style, and that if women dare to approach that style, they break divine law and commit great sin and wrong? It is a presumption and insult which women everywhere should resent."

She then took Mr. Talmage himself to task for disregarding Moses's command that men should put fringes and blue ribbons on their garments. To this, her clerical critic could find no answer.

But Mrs. Bloomer was not satisfied to let the subject drop. She had more to say. "If divine law or vengeance is ever visited upon woman because of the cut of her garments, it will be upon the wearer of the suicidal long heavy skirts, instead of upon those who have rid themselves of the grievous burden."

That winter chanced to be a cold one and it became fashionable among older men to supplement their winter garments by wearing a shawl. Some newspapers made sarcastic comments about this and published satirical cartoons.

Mrs. Bloomer's attitude was unexpected. "There is a class of men who seem to think it their especial business to supervise the wardrobes of both men and women, and if any dare to depart from their ideas of propriety, they criticize."

In her view, shawls should be entirely banned. They were inconvenient and injurious articles of apparel, owing to their requiring both hands to keep them on and thereby tending to contract the chest and cause stooping shoulders. But, if worn at all, men had the same right to them that women had. If they found shawls convenient, that was enough, and no one had a right to object to their wearing them because women wore shawls.

Mrs. Bloomer had strong support from Mrs. Stanton in her skirmishes with the clergy. Elizabeth had never forgc ten her disillusioning experience as a girl over the ungrateful young man trained for the ministry with the money she had helped to raise. Annoyed by the hostile attitude of so many divines towards the cause of Women's Rights, she made a startling speech at a meeting of the Women's Temperance Society.

"Inasmuch as charity begins at home, let us withdraw our mite from all associations for sending the Gospel across the ocean, for the education of young men for the ministry, for the building up of a theological aristocracy, and gorgeous temples to the unknown God, and devote ourselves to the poor and needy around us. Let us feed and clothe the hungry and naked, gather children into schools, and provide reading-rooms and decent homes for young men and women thrown alone upon the world. Good schools and homes, where the young could ever be surrounded by an atmosphere of purity and virtue, would do much more to prevent immorality and crime in our cities than all the churches in the land could ever possibly do towards the regeneration of the multitude sunk in poverty, ignorance, and vice."

VIII

TRIUMPHANT IN NEW YORK

IN FEBRUARY, 1853, Mrs. Bloomer went to address a meeting in the Metropolitan Hall, New York. It was packed with some three thousand people and many were turned away. Thanks to the publicity attracted by the Bloomer Costume, she had become a figure of world-wide fame and the New Yorkers were eager and curious to see her.

The correspondent of the *New York Tribune* gave his report the heading: "Great Gathering of the Women of New York", and wrote: "The Women's Grand Temperance Demonstration last night was a most brilliant and successful affair. The audience which assembled on that occasion to welcome Mrs. Bloomer and her assistants in the cause of Temperance was almost as large and fully as respectable as the audience that nightly greeted Jenny Lind and Catharine Hays during their engagement in the Hall.

"Mrs. Bloomer was attired in a dark-brown changeable tunic with a kilt descending to just below her knees, the skirt of which was trimmed with rows of black velvet. Her pantaloons were of the same texture and trimmed in the same style. She wore gaiters. Her head-dress was cherry and black. Her dress had a large, open corsage, with bands of velvet over the white chemisette in which was fixed a diamond stud pin. She wore flowing sleeves, tight undersleeves, and black mitts. Her whole attire was both rich and plain in appearance.

"The audience was a smiling one, some smiled at the novelty of the occasion, others with admiration; the latter, judging from the twinkling of eyes and clapping of hands, were in the majority. While some evidently writhed under the application of the lash for their disregard of the principles of temperance, others enjoyed the rigor of the infliction and manifested their satisfaction by applause."

After her success in New York, Mrs. Bloomer together with Miss Anthony set out on a lecture tour of the State, holding meetings in Brooklyn, Poughkeepsie, Sing Sing, Hudson, Troy, Cohoes, Utica, Syracuse, Rochester, Lockport, Buffalo, and other places along the Hudson River and the line of the Central Railroad. She enjoyed, she wrote in her diary, "jaunting through some of the cities and villages of the beautiful Hudson, seeing much of the grand and beautiful in nature, and making the acquaintance of some of the choice spirits of that section of the State".

Mrs. Bloomer described the closing meeting of the campaign at Buffalo thus: "Townsend Hall was crowded at an early hour by the curious and interested portions of the community, who came together to see the women who had made themselves notorious by their boldness in daring to face a city audience, and to listen to the strange and 'funny things' they might utter on the worn and rather unpopular subject of temperance. The capacity of the hall is said to be sufficient to seat a thousand. Every spot where a standing place could be had was occupied, and many went away unable to gain admittance.

"Steps were immediately taken by some friends here to secure a hall for another meeting the next evening. Townsend Hall and the American Hall were both engaged, so the Eagle Street Theatre was secured instead; and last night, for the first time in many years, I attended a theatre not as a looker-on, but as an actor in the play. I don't know the capacity of the theatre, but it was estimated that fully one thousand two hundred persons were present, the body of the house and the lower gallery being densely filled, while many occupied the upper gallery and the rostrum. The audience appeared interested and were for the most part quiet and attentive."

Mrs. Bloomer's remarkable progress as a public speaker deserves stressing. In less than a year from her début in the spring of 1852, she had become the most publicized lecturer in the country. Within a few years, she prophesied, it would be no strange thing to see women merchants, book-keepers, shoemakers, cabinetmakers, jewellers, booksellers, typesetters, editors, publishers, lawyers, surgeons, physicians, and even preachers.

Woman had a right to vote, to hold office, and so rule over men. Deborah ruled Israel for forty years wisely and well. No one called in question the right of Queen Victoria to rule over her kingdom, notwithstanding there were men in it. If it was right for Victoria to sit on the throne of England, it was right for any American woman to occupy the Presidential chair in Washington. All that was needed were votes enough to elevate her to that position of honour and trust, and sufficient ability to discharge its duties. "Of the latter requisite, judging from some of those who have already occupied that seat, no great amount is demanded!"

The mark of public esteem which pleased Mrs. Bloomer most was when in 1853 she was engaged as the orator at Hartford, Connecticut, for the Fourth of July celebrations. At ten o'clock in the morning, the procession formed in front of the Union Church, and the "Good Templars" and the "Sons of Temperance" in the regalia of their orders, led by a band of music and followed by the people, proceeded to a grove where seats and a handsomely decorated stand had been prepared for the occasion.

Mrs. Bloomer was, of course, in a Bloomer Costume. To her delight, she found a committee of ladies similarly dressed waiting in the grove to escort her to the seat of honour. It was the first time anywhere a woman had been asked to deliver the public oration on the national feast day.

"Although the women of the Revolution," she pointed out, "had toiled along with the men for independence and freedom, yet they failed, when the struggle was over, to secure an equality in those rights and duties which are the common birthright of a!'. May their daughters of the present generation be more fortunate in their struggle for rights so long withheld!"

Homer, Amelia's birthplace, was not far from Hartford, so she took the opportunity of revisiting the old home she had last seen when six years old. The news of her arrival spread round the small town very quickly, and people waved from windows and came running out of their houses to shake her by the hand and say how proud they were of Homer's famous daughter.

She was overwhelmed by her welcome, and especially glad when she learned that quite a number of mothers

94

had dressed their daughters in Bloomer Costume, and wore the short dress when doing their housework.

The leading citizen, Mr. William Sherman, and his wife called on the Bloomers at the hotel where they were lunching, and begged them to stay the night with them, so that they might all have an opportunity of hearing her speak.

Mrs. Bloomer, though tired after the Fourth of July celebrations, willingly agreed. Once again, she repeated her success. People had to be turned away from the large church hall belonging to the Presbyterians where she spoke and, rather than disappoint them, she remained another night and addressed a second meeting. "Though I interspersed my lecture pretty freely with women's rights, or rather I might say with women's wrongs," wrote Amelia in her diary, "no one seemed at all alarmed; but if we may believe the assertion of the people, new trains of thought were awakened and a most favourable impression made on the minds of the community."

The following morning, the Bloomers took the stage homewards, but as they were waiting for the boat at Glen Haven, they were approached by a Dr. Jackson who told Amelia that he conducted a water cure sanatorium on the beautiful shores of the Skaneateles Lake. Would Mr. and Mrs. Bloomer be his guests for the night there, so that Amelia could talk to the patients? She had not the heart to refuse when he revealed that owing to his advice most of them wore the costume she advocated.

She spoke in a large sitting-room in the evening. The medical staff and even the servants crowded it to overflowing. Among her listeners was a Judge Osborn from the near-by small town of Scott. He had been visiting his wife, who was a patient, and had stayed on so as to

95

be able to listen to Mrs. Bloomer. He was so impressed that he asked her to go to Scott and speak on the Friday evening, instead of returning home.

Mrs. Bloomer felt that if she did not refuse this request she might well find herself lecturing for the rest of the month. The judge, however, was persistent and Amelia gave way, for she afterwards told Dexter that a Judge sympathetic to women's rights was a rare bird indeed, to be tamed and kept friendly at all costs.

These lecture tours were beginning to tell on Amelia's health and Dexter was worried. "Small in person and fragile in health," he wrote, "she had been enabled to endure so much only by her indomitable courage and spirit of perseverance which ever controlled all her actions." They had both been impressed with Dr. Jackson's sanatorium and its delightful situation on the lakeside, so she spent some weeks there resting as a patient. Though she rested her body, she did not rest her mind, but spent a great deal of her time writing articles and preparing new lectures.

One of the chief reasons why Amelia had allowed herself to be persuaded by Dexter into entering the sanatorium was because she wanted to be in the best of health when three organizations she supported held meetings in New York all in the same week in September—the Anti-Slavery Society, the Whole World's Temperance Convention and the Women's Rights Convention.

Never before had the three causes most unpopular with the conservative camp dared to invade New York in such force. The newspapers predicted trouble—and trouble there was.

IX

BATTLE ON BROADWAY

THE LEADING papers in the United States in 1853 were the *Tribune,* the *Herald,* the *Times,* the *Evening Post* and the *Express.* They were all edited by men of great ability. The *Tribune* was independent and liberal in outlook and had for Editor, Horace Greeley, who was sympathetic to the Women's Rights Movement. The *Herald* under James Gordon Bennett led the opposition, and had no scruples when it came to attacking the advocates of reform. The *Times* edited by Henry J. Raymond was in the same camp, but more restrained. The *Evening Post* under the fair-minded William Cullen Bryant supported the women, whilst the *Express* abused them in similar style to the *Herald.*

On the first Sunday in September, the Anti-Slavery Society opened its proceedings with a religious meeting attended by over five thousand people at which Antoinette Brown, soon to become the first woman ever to be ordained as a minister, preached the sermon. This took place in the Metropolitan Hall where Amelia Bloomer had spoken the year before. It was claimed to be the largest congregation that had ever gathered within the walls of any building in New York.

This event angered the conservative section of the religious Press, whilst James Gordon Bennett of the *Herald* described Miss Brown's behaviour as a calculated piece of bravado which must not be allowed to recur.

Consequently, there were noisy interruptions next day when the Whole World's Temperance Convention held its meeting also in the Metropolitan Hall. This was attended by men and women delegates, and was addressed by Antoinette Brown and other leading feminists, including Mrs. Bloomer.

The Rev. W. H. Channing took the opportunity to defend Miss Brown. Jenny Lind had sung "I know that my Redeemer liveth" from that very platform. The packed audience had applauded, and no one had criticized her for doing so. Miss Brown in her sermon the previous day had uttered similar sentiments. What was there unfeminine or revolting in her preaching "the truth which Jenny Lind may sing without objection and amid universal applause?"

Two days later, on Wednesday, September 7th, the feminists themselves assembled in the "Tabernacle" on Broadway to hold their Women's Rights Convention. Long before the morning session was due to open, the hall was packed with over three thousand people. Amongst them were the hired agents of James Gordon Bennett who had been instructed to do all they could to wreck the proceedings.

Mrs. Lucretia Mott, who was in the Chair, welcomed the presence of two delegates from overseas, Mary Jackson and Mathilde Franceska Anneké, representing England and Germany, and then called upon the first speaker, William Lloyd Garrison, the veteran Abolitionist campaigner.

In the early days of his career Garrison had once been mobbed and dragged through the streets of Boston tied to the end of a rope, only escaping with his life through courageous women supporters forming a bulwark of protection around him with their own bodies. He had sat silent in the gallery during the World's Anti-Slavery Convention in London of 1840, when they had refused to recognize the women delegates from America. He had sent a letter of encouragement to the first Women's Rights Convention of 1848 in Seneca Falls. And now in return for Antoinette Brown's support the previous Sunday at the Anti-Slavery Convention, he had come to speak at the women's own meeting.

He began by asking what had brought them there. It was because justice was being outraged. In all ages, men had regarded women as inferior to themselves and had robbed them of their rights. They were now contesting that tyranny. He had been derisively called a Women's Rights' Man. He knew no such distinction. "I claim to be a Human Rights' Man, and wherever there is a human being, I see God-given rights inherent in that being whatever may be the sex or complexion."

At this juncture, the paid hecklers drowned his words with insults and violent stamping on the floor. Garrison had been forewarned to expect trouble. Contemptuously he shouted back at his interrupters that the Women's Rights Movement did not want the compliments of the *New York Herald* or the *Times* or the *Express*. "If you want the compliments of such journals, you must be bad enough to take a place among the very lowest of the human race. Let us rejoice at this manifestation of their hate, for it proves this cause to be a righteous one, and in due season it will triumph."

He was followed by two other male speakers, throughout whose speeches the rowdies continued their barrage of abuse. Then came Lucy Stone, one of the most gifted of the feminist orators. When a girl, she had begged her father to send her to college. He had refused, so she had gone out to work in order to earn enough money to pay her fees at Oberlin College, where she had graduated in 1847. She had then devoted her life to lecturing in favour of the abolition of slavery and the attainment of women's rights. She was in 1855 to marry the brother of Elizabeth Blackwell, the first woman ever to obtain a medical degree from a college. Henry Blackwell, a prominent advocate of equality between the sexes, agreed that Lucy should continue to be known by her maiden name after marriage. His brother, Samuel, married Antoinette Brown.

Lucy was regarded as a martyr by the feminists, as she had refused to pay her taxes until she was given the vote. As a result, the authorities had seized her New Jersey property and sold it. This was the woman who, unruffled and smiling, faced the hecklers. She was dressed in a Bloomer costume which happened to particularly suit her slight figure. It was said that she and Mrs. Bloomer were the two best advertisements for the new style. Her favourite story of the many comments it attracted concerned the reaction she received when in Louisville, Kentucky. A Negro woman at the public pump had put her hands on her hips, awaiting Lucy's approach, and had asked: "Be you one of them theatre women?" A passing male had shouted the reply: "She's put her petticoats up the spout so now she has to go without!"

There was a commanding air about Lucy Stone that compelled attention, and after a few moments the derisive applause of the hecklers that greeted her died away, and they listened.

Proudly, she listed the achievements of her sex to date. Already, there were three successful women physicians practising in New York and a female medical college where many more were being trained. Women were becoming merchants and making money. The energy and ability for business of many had repaired the losses of their less competent husbands. A Mrs. Tyndal of Lowell, Massachusettes, had made herself rich by running a ladies' shoe store. She had said to herself, "What is to hinder me from going into this business? I should know ladies' shoes, whether they are good or bad, and what price they can bring. The ladies would support me." And so they had.

Lucy Stone went on to reveal that as a result of Antoinette Brown's successful sermon in the Metropolitan Hall the previous Sunday "some men in New York, knowing that they can hear the word of God from a woman, as well as from a man, have called her to be their pastor, and she is to be ordained this month".

Applause from the women, and stamping of feet, hissing, and shouts of derision from the rowdies interrupted Miss Stone. She waited for the din to subside, then told them that in Chicago a woman had been elected cashier of a bank with a majority of three hundred over her male opponent. Women could be editors, too. She named Mrs. Bloomer, who was sitting in the audience, and two others—Paulina W. Davis and Mrs. Nichols—who were behind her on the platform. Perhaps one day even the *New York Herald* might have a lady editor!

The *Herald* hired representatives could not let this pass without protest, and such a tumult broke out that Horace Greeley, Editor of the *Tribune*, who was

present, made an attempt to quell it. In the words of
the reporter from the *Times*, going up into the gallery,
Mr. Greeley "remonstrated with the sibilating gentlemen, and a great rumpus was raised. Some cheered the
peace-maker, others hissed and all proceedings were
interrupted."

Horace Greeley's own *Tribune* stated next day that
one ought to thank the disturbers "for so stirring the
souls of the speakers that their words came gushing
forth from their lips with exceeding fluency and power.
It was never before so transparent that a hiss or a black-
guard yell was the only answer that the case admitted
of, and when Lucy Stone closed the discussion with
some pungent, yet pathetic remarks on the sort of opposition that had been manifest, it was evident that if any
of the rowdies had an ant-hole in the bottom of his
boot, he would inevitably have sunk through it and
disappeared for ever."

James Gordon Bennett published an angry attack on
the Convention in his *Herald*. "The assemblage of
rampant women which convened at the 'Tabernacle'
last night—unsexed in mind all of them, and many in
habiliments—publicly propounded the doctrine that
they should be allowed to step out of the appropriate
spheres to the neglect of those duties which both human
and divine law have assigned to them . . . Is the world
to be depopulated? Are there to be no more children?"

He went on to accuse Mrs. Bloomer, Lucy Stone and
their associates of pocketing all the money they could
wring from "the barren fools who can be found in any
community eager to grasp at any doctrine which is
novel, no matter how outrageous it may be". This they
did by collections for fugitive slaves, and selling "Thrill-
ing Narratives" of the adventures of the latter when
making their escapes. Recently, he claimed, the women

had discovered that the great body of their audiences came only to be amused and had imposed an admission charge. "Lucy Stone, who is a shrewd Yankee, has gone a step further, and in her management of the Women's Rights Convention has provided for season tickets to be had at the 'extremely low price of two shillings'."

On its second day, the morning session of the Convention opened at ten o'clock. Once again, there was standing room only soon after the doors of the Tabernacle opened at nine.

Lucretia Mott, who took the chair, began by claiming that the uproar and confusion amid which the proceedings had closed on the previous evening, although much to be regretted, yet when viewed in the proper perspective might provide them with good reason for congratulating themselves. In spite of all the rowdiness and the hooligan attempt to break up the meeting not a scream had been heard from any woman. The so-called weaker sex had thus shown fortitude under provocation, and this was because of their strong belief in the truth and justice of their cause.

A man, who gave his name as H. K. Root, then rose from his seat in the hall and said that he had three good reasons for not giving women the vote. Mrs. Mott invited him to take the rostrum which he did. His first reason, he said, was that God had laid down that man should rule. He was sure that if men now gave up their rights to women, some great calamity would fall upon them. His second reason was the law of physical force —because man's strength was greater than woman's. His third was: "If woman says we shall vote, and man says she shan't, he is in duty bound to maintain what he says. If he says that she shan't, that is reason enough why she should not." And with this extraordinary piece of homespun logic, Mr. Root returned to his seat to the clapping of the anti-feminists.

The next speaker was Mrs. Frances Dana Gage, a great friend of Mrs. Bloomer, who then enjoyed world-wide fame for her poems written under the name of "Aunt Fanny". She described how that morning when leaving her boarding-house, someone had said to her: "So you are ready armed and equipped to go and fight the men!" She had been truly sorry to hear this, as she had no quarrel with men. She was a daughter, a sister, a wife and a mother, and in all these relationships she lived in harmony with man. The bad laws and customs of society were their only enemies.

Mrs. Gage was followed by Dr. Harriot K. Hunt, the pioneer woman physician who had gained notoriety by being refused admittance to the Harvard Medical School in 1847 and again in 1850. She related how in October, 1851, she had gone to pay her taxes in Boston. "Going into the Assessor's office, I saw a tall, thin, weak, stupid-looking Irish boy. It was near election time. He held in his hand a document which I found on enquiry was one of naturalization; and this hopeful son of Erin was made a citizen of the United States, and he could have a voice in determining the destinies of this mighty nation, whilst thousands of intellectual women, daughters of the soil, no matter how respectable or what amount of taxes they paid, were forced to be dumb!"

Dr. Hunt went on to say that she had meditated on what she had seen and, when paying her taxes in 1852, she had handed the Treasurer a written protest against being compelled to do so whilst having no vote. She would go on doing this every year so long as she lived.

Although the hired hecklers were all present, their interruptions during the morning session were perfunctory and spasmodic, but when the meeting reassembled after lunch, the appearance on the platform of Sojourner Truth, a tall, coloured woman, well known in anti-slavery circles, was the signal for a fresh outburst of rowdiness. She combined in her person the elements of humanity most hated by the opposition. She was black and she was a woman. She had once been a slave in the State of New York. Her back was scarred from the whippings she had received. She was eighty-two years old (she was to live to the age of over a hundred and ten), could neither read nor write, but had rare intelligence and commonsense. Standing there unperturbed in a simple grey dress and wearing on her head a white turban, surmounted with an ancient sun-bonnet, she ignored all the insults that were hurled at her. She had a quiet, impressive dignity. She looked almost with pity at her tormentors, and when at last they were unwillingly quelled into near silence by her all-penetrating gaze, she spoke.

"Wall, chilern, whan dar is so much racket dar must be somethin' out of kilter. I tink dat 'twixt de niggers of de Souf and de womin at de Norf, all talkin' 'bout rights, de white men will be in a fix pretty soon. But what's all dis here talkin' 'bout?

"Dat man ober dar say dat womin needs to be helped into carriages, and lifted ober ditches, and to hab de best place everywhar. Nobody eber helps me into carriages, or ober mud-puddles, or gibs me any best place!" And raising herself to her full height and her voice to a dramatic pitch, she asked: "And a'n't I a woman? Look at me! Look at my arm!" She bared her right arm to the shoulder, showing the muscular power she still possessed despite her age.

"I have ploughed, and planted, and gathered into barns, and no man could head me! And a'n't I a woman? I could work as much and eat as much as a man—when I could get it—and bear de lash as well! And a'n't I a woman? I have borne thirteen children, and seen 'em mos' all sold off to slavery, and when I cried out with my mother's grief, none but Jesus heard me! And a'n't I a woman?

"Den dat little man in black dar, he say womin can't have as much rights as men, 'cause Christ wan't a woman! Whar did your Christ come from?"

Rolling thunder could not have stilled that crowd, an eye-witness of the scene has recorded, as did those deep, wonderful tones. With outstretched arms and eyes of fire Sojourner Truth repeated, raising her voice still louder: "Whar did your Christ come from? From God and a woman! Man had nothin' to do wid Him.

" 'Bleeged to ye for hearin' me, and now ole Sojourner han't got nothin' more to say."

The hecklers were stunned into silence as she sat down, but they soon recovered and became progressively noisier with the speakers that followed.

Mrs. Bloomer proposed that a committee should be appointed to prepare an address to the women of Great Britain and the Continent of Europe, setting forth their objects, and inviting their co-operation in the struggle to achieve them.

A Mr. W. L. Gavin seconded this, but his speech was completely obliterated by a storm of hisses from the hecklers. At this point, Isaac C. Pray, a journalist well-known for his bitter attacks on the feminists, asked permission to speak from Mrs. Mott. She agreed after some hesitation, for she naturally expected that he would make a furious attack on the resolution.

The rowdies cheered, but their premature enthusiasm soon turned to rage as they listened. Until a short time previously, admitted Mr. Pray, he had been an opponent of the women on the platform, writing articles ridiculing them in a leading New York journal—the journal "which gives the cue to the hisses in the gallery". But he had now ceased writing for that publication, and had spent some time seriously studying the case for and against the Women's Rights Movement.

"The result is that I have entirely changed my opinion. I know not only that my former opinion was wrong, but that this movement is one which you cannot stop. This cause has been the butt of all the ridicule I could command. There is not a lady on this platform whom my pen has not assailed, and now I come to make all the reparation in my power, by thus raising my voice on behalf of them and the cause committed to their hands."

The hirelings of Mr. Pray's former Editor roared and stamped and howled abuse. A burly ruffian rushed down from the gallery brandishing a cudgel. The male supporters of the feminists restrained him. As it was inconsistent with Lucretia Mott's Quaker principles to call upon the police for the forcible suppression of the mob, she vacated the Chair, inviting Mrs. Ernestine L. Rose to take her place.

This beautiful Jewess was the right person to handle such a situation. Daughter of a Rabbi, she had fought against oppression in her native Poland as a girl. Escaping to London, she had met there and married an American, William L. Rose. After reaching New York in 1836, she had toured the country lecturing on her native Poland's plight. Her eloquence and wit had brought her fame, and she had been one of the first to join the Women's Rights Movement.

Calling on the police to restore order, Mrs. Rose prorogued the Convention till the evening for its final session. But the Mayor of New York had no use for feminists. He had deliberately sent few police to maintain order and when the doors reopened in the evening, they made no attempt to prevent the hecklers from entering the Broadway Tabernacle.

Hoping that the hoodlums would at least give a foreigner a hearing, Mrs. Ernestine L. Rose arranged for the first speaker to be a German lady, Madame Mathilde Anneké, Editress of a Liberal Women's Rights newspaper which had been suppressed in Germany. She spoke in her native tongue. Mrs. Rose translated her remarks into English. Madame Anneké said that she had hastened to the Convention to enjoy the blessings of free speech in a republic. She had heard so much of freedom in America that she could hardly express her astonishment at what she had witnessed.

"I wish to say only a few words. On the other side of the Atlantic, there is no freedom of any kind, and we have not even the right to freedom of speech. But can it be that here, too, there are tyrants who violate the individual right to express opinions on any subject? And do you call yourselves republicans?"

Once again the uproar was such that neither of the two women could be heard. Wendell Phillips, who had pleaded in London in 1840 for the women to be admitted to the World's Anti-Slavery Convention, leapt to his feet. He was a magnificent-looking man with tremendous personality and authority. "Allow me to say a few words, purely as a matter of self respect which you owe to yourselves," he shouted at the interrupters. "We are citizens of a great country, which extended a welcome to Kossuth, and this New York audience is now looking upon a noble woman who stood by his side in the battlefields of Hungary—one who has faced the cannon of Francis Joseph of Austria for the rights of the people. Is this the welcome you give a woman who has proved her gallantry and wishes to say a few words to you of the feeling with which she is impressed towards this cause? I know, fellow citizens, that you will hear her."

This appeal quelled the hecklers into an uneasy truce and Mathilde Anneké, with Ernestine Rose as interpreter, resumed her speech. She had read for the first time in a newspaper about this Convention. She had rejoiced to know that they were claiming equal rights not only for American women, but also for their sisters in Germany. Women in that country had long desired freedom. In America, she had expected to find freedom of speech, but what she had experienced that day in this hall on Broadway had saddened her. For if American men betrayed their heritage by denying their own women freedom of speech, what hope was there for the women of the world elsewhere?"

But the mob would not listen to any more. They had been promised a bonus if they broke up the Convention before its scheduled end. They went mad—they bawled and bellowed—they howled and stamped.

Again, Mrs. Rose called on the police to preserve order. "As citizens of New York, we have a right to their protection, for we pay our money for it. If the police are not able to keep order, I call upon the meeting to help them."

At this, one of the hecklers named Elliott, jumped on to the platform and shouted that Mrs. Rose was inciting her supporters to violence. The confusion reached a climax. It was impossible for anyone wishing to speak to be heard. And so, reluctantly, Mrs. Rose closed the Convention.

Next day, Horace Greeley's sympathetic *Tribune* commented: "We do not know whether any of the *gentlemen* who have succeeded in breaking up the Women's Rights Convention will ever feeled ashamed of their hostility, but we have little doubt that some of them will live to understand their own folly . . . Nothing is so good for a weak and unpopular movement as this sort of opposition. The consequences will be that the mass of people throughout the country who might otherwise not know of its existence will have their attention called and their sympathies enlisted on its behalf."

The *Tribune* was right. The new movement gained much support, and within three months a further Convention was being held in Rochester, at which Mrs. Bloomer was elected a Vice-President. A circular was widely distributed, inviting all to attend, if interested in furthering "the just and equal rights of women". It stated that the Conventions held for several years past in different States had answered their end of arousing public attention. The time had come for calling upon the people to act.

"Thousands of the best men and women are asking such questions as these: 1. Why should not work be paid for according to the quality of the work done, and not the sex of the worker? 2. How shall we open for women's energies new spheres of well-remunerated industry? 3. Why should not wives, equally with husbands, be entitled to their own earnings? 4. Why should not widows, equally with widowers, become by law the legal guardians, as they certainly are by nature the natural guardians, of their own children? 5. On what just grounds do the laws make a distinction between men and women in regard to the ownership of property, inheritance, and the administration of estates? 6. Why should woman, any more than man, be taxed without representation? 7. Why may not women claim to be tried by a jury of their peers, with exactly the same right as men claim to be and actually are? 8. If women need the protection of the law, and are subject to the penalties of the law equally with men, why should they not have an equal influence in making the laws?

"And finally, if governments, according to our National Declaration of Independence, derive their just powers from the consent of the governed, why should women, any more than men, be governed without their own consent, and why, therefore, is not woman's right to suffrage precisely equal to man?

"For the purpose of finding out practical answers to these and similar questions, and making suitable arrangements to bring the existing wrongs of women before the Legislature at its next session, we, the undersigned, do earnestly request the men and women of the Commonwealth to assemble in Convention, in the City of Rochester, on Wednesday, November 30th, and Thursday, December 1st, 1853."

It is interesting to note, when studying the original document, that the first bold signature to this clarion call is that of Elizabeth Cady Stanton.

As a result of the Rochester meeting, two committees were appointed: one to prepare an address to the capitalists and industrialists of New York State on the best modes of employing and remunerating women; and another, consisting of Mrs. Stanton, Mrs. Rose, and Miss Anthony, to prepare an address to the Legislature, and to ask a special hearing to consider the whole subject of the just and equal rights of women.

From all this one can see that it was not for the want of trying that women did not get the vote generally in the States until nearly seventy years later. But much had been achieved largely due to the publicity lavished on the Bloomer Costume. This gave the women's cause a great impetus and advanced the fulfilment of its aims by many years.

"If the dress drew the crowds that came to hear me, it was well," Mrs. Bloomer wrote in her diary. "They heard the message I brought them, and it has borne abundant fruit. Until the papers had ceased writing squibs at my expense, I wore no other costume. . . .

"Mrs. Stanton ably defended the new style. She continued to wear it at home and abroad, on the lecture platform and in the social parlour, for two or three years; and then the pressure brought to bear upon her by her father and other friends was so great that she finally yielded to their wishes and returned to long skirts."

In fact, most of the feminists wore the costume for only about three years. Elizabeth Smith Miller, the originator, adhered to it for nearly seven years under most trying conditions. Whilst her father was in Congress, she wore it at many fashionable dinners and receptions, but she had to endure much open rudeness and ridicule.

"Such is the tyranny of custom," Mrs. Stanton has recorded, "that to escape constant observation, criticism, ridicule, and persecution, one after another gladly went back to the old slavery, and sacrificed freedom of movement to repose. I have never wondered since that the Chinese women allow their daughters' feet to be encased in iron shoes, nor that the Hindoo widows walk calmly to the funeral pyre.

"We knew the Bloomer Costume never could be generally becoming, as it required a perfection of form, limbs, and feet, such as few possess, and we who wore it also knew that it was not artistic.

"Though the martyrdom proved too much for us who had so many other measures to press on public conscience, yet no experiment is lost, however evanescent, that rouses thought to the injurious consequences of the present style of dress.

"We had no reason to hope that pantaloons would do more for us than they have done for man himself. The Negro slave enjoys the most unlimited freedom in his attire, not surpassed even by the fashions of Eden in its palmiest days; yet in spite of his dress and his manhood, he is a slave still.

"Was the old Roman in his toga less of a man than he is now in swallow-tail and tights?"

But the most important reason why Mrs. Bloomer and her circle left off wearing the short dress was given by Amelia many years later in her old age.

"We all felt that the dress was drawing attention from what we thought to be of far greater importance —the question of woman's right to better education, to a wider field of employment, to better remuneration for her labour, and to the ballot for the protection of her rights. In the minds of some people the short dress and woman's rights were inseparably connected. With us, the dress was but an incident, and we were not willing to sacrifice greater questions to it."

It is interesting to note that Elizabeth Cady Stanton herself once suggested to her feminist friends that they should reform the Bloomer Costume by leaving off wearing the pantaloons and having just a short skirt to the knees with stockings in winter and bare legs in summer, but in this she was ahead of her time and her suggestion was not adopted.

Years later, in 1869, she wrote in the Woman Suffrage Association newspaper, *The Revolution,* that she believed the day would come when the sexes were dressed as nearly alike as possible. She mentioned how a young New York woman had travelled all over

Europe and America in male attire and, thanks to it, had enjoyed a masculine independence and security.

"When we have a voice in legislation, we shall dress as we please," stated Mrs. Stanton, "and if, by concealing our sex, we find that we, too, can roam up and down the earth in safety, we shall keep our womanhood a profound secret."

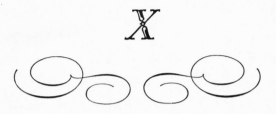

SUSAN B. ANTHONY

MENTION HAS already been made of Susan Brownell Anthony, Mrs. Bloomer's principal companion on her early lecturing tours. Hers is one of the greatest names in the story of the Women's Rights Movement. She was two years younger than Amelia and five years the junior of Mrs. Stanton, and came of sturdy New England stock.

Susan's father, though a Quaker, became one of the wealthiest men in Washington County and he had his daughter educated by private tutors. He offended the Quakers by marrying a Baptist wife, and for this offence was disowned and told that he could only be received into the fellowship again if he declared himself "sorry" for his crime at a full meeting. When he rose to speak, he said he was "sorry" that the rules of the society were such that, in marrying the woman he loved, he had committed offence! But as he had admitted that he was "sorry" for something, he was taken back into the body of the faithful.

Mr. Anthony, despite his wealth, made it a matter

of conscience to bring up his children to be self-supporting. Susan chose the profession of teacher, for which she proved well suited as she had a gift for imparting knowledge. She also had a gift for maintaining discipline, although she looked so gentle. On one occasion, a certain school at Center Falls had become notorious for the bullying activities of a strapping lad who terrorized his male teachers and drove them out. Susan went in their place. She looked very meek to the barbarian of fifteen and he soon began his antics. He was called to the platform, told to lay aside his jacket, and thereupon with much astonishment received from the mild Quaker maiden a good birching. Thus Susan departed from her principles, but not from the school.

At the time of the first Women's Rights Convention of 1848, Miss Anthony was teaching at a school in the little village of Canajoharie in the state of New York. She was now twenty-eight, tired of schoolteaching, but not quite sure where her life's work lay. She was amused rather than impressed by what she read about the Convention, but when she went home to Rochester on vacation, she learnt that her mother, father and sister had all attended the meetings. She was astonished to hear that they had been so stirred by the speeches that they had signed the Declaration of Sentiments and the Resolutions. They told her, too, that her cousin, Sarah Anthony Burtis, had acted as Secretary of the Convention.

Mr. and Mrs. Anthony spoke with such admiration about Mrs. Stanton with her black curls and ruddy cheeks, and about Mrs. Mott with her Quaker cap and kerchief of finest muslin, both speaking so superbly and looking so striking, that Susan began to think more about the subject of women's rights and to wish that she could one day meet these two extraordinary women.

116

She believed in equal rights for men and women herself already, and had long thought it unfair for women teachers to be paid less than men. But having been brought up a Quaker, she was not certain about wanting the vote for her sex. Her father, Daniel Anthony, did not vote; like the other Quakers he considered it wrong to vote for any political party that supported war.

Susan did not return to her teaching post, because her father had taken over an insurance business in Syracuse and he wanted her to help manage his farm while he was away. As a result, she became friendly with a group of Rochester Liberals and Abolitionists and soon found herself in complete sympathy with their ideas and aims. She also became an active member of the society known as the "Daughters of Temperance", and consequently became a great friend of Mrs. Bloomer.

In May, 1851, Susan went to stay with Amelia in Seneca Falls so that she could attend the Anti-Slavery meeting held there by the famous Abolitionists, George Thompson and William Lloyd Garrison. "These gentlemen were my guests," wrote Mrs. Stanton in her reminiscences. "Walking home, after the adjournment, we met Mrs. Bloomer and Miss Anthony on the corner of the street, waiting to greet us. There Susan stood, with her good, earnest face and genial smile, dressed in grey delaine, hat and all the same colour, relieved with pale blue ribbons, the perfection of neatness and sobriety. I liked her thoroughly, and why I did not at once invite her home with me to dinner I do not know. She accuses me of that neglect, and has never forgiven me, as she wished to see and hear all she could of our noble friends."

From this chance meeting began a life-long friendship, destined to have far-reaching effects on the future lives of American women. At that time, Mrs. Stanton was finding life very difficult trying to cope with her high-spirited boys on her own. To quote her own words, "Miss Anthony, my good angel, pushed and goaded me to work that but for her partnership I should never have accomplished. It has been said that I forged the thunderbolts, and that she fired them. Perhaps all this is in a measure true. With the cares of a large family, I might in time, like too many women, have become wholly absorbed in a narrow family selfishness, had not my friend been continually exploring new fields for missionary labours."

Whenever Elizabeth saw the stately Quaker girl coming across her lawn, she knew that some happy convocation of the sons of Adam was to be set by the ears by one of their appeals or resolutions. Susan's little portmanteau, stuffed with facts, would be opened, and there they had statistics of women robbed of their property, shut out of some college, half paid for their work; the reports of some disgraceful trial: "injustice enough to turn any woman's thoughts from mending stockings and making puddings".

Then the two women would get out their pens and write articles for the papers, or a petition to the legislature; indite letters to the faithful here and there; stir up the women in Ohio, Pennsylvania or Massachusetts; call on *The Lily, The Liberator* or *The Standard* to remember white women's wrongs as well as those of the slave.

They never met without issuing a pronouncement on some question. In thought and sympathy they were one, and in division of labour they exactly complemented each other. "In writing, we did better work than either could alone. While Susan was slow and analytical in composition, I was rapid and synthetic. I am the better

118

writer—she, the better critic. She supplied the facts and statistics—I, the philosophy and rhetoric. Together, we have made arguments that have stood unshaken through the storm of long years—arguments that no one has answered. Our speeches may be considered the united product of our two brains."

Privately, Elizabeth and Susan indulged freely in criticism of each other and hotly contended their differences. But in public they always seemed to agree.

Night after night, by an old-fashioned fireplace, they plotted and planned the coming agitation. Every right to enter a college, to study a profession, to labour in some new industry or to advocate a reform measure, was contended for, inch by inch. One of their earliest victories came in February, 1852, when for the first time anywhere in the world women were admitted to medical studies. Arrangements were made for a complete course of medical instruction by six Professors to be given in a special department of the Boston Medical School—thereafter known as the 'New England Female Medical School'.

Miss Anthony first carried her flag of rebellion into State conventions of teachers and there fought, almost single-handed, the battle for equality. She was a rapid speaker, quick-witted and keen in debate.

She was always equal to an emergency. "When suddenly called upon to speak to some women assembled at a station," Mrs. Stanton once confided, "I was filled with consternation and appealed to her to go first, and without a moment's hesitation she filled five minutes with some appropriate words, and inspired me with thought and courage to follow."

It was said of the two women that each did not so much supplement the other's deficiencies as augment the other's eccentricities; that they often stimulated each other's aggressiveness and, at the same time, dimmed each other's discretion; that whatever might be the imprudent utterances of the one, or the impolitic methods of the other, the animating motives of both were as white as the light; and that the good that they did was by design, and the harm by accident.

A male opponent declared that he knew of no two more pertinacious incendiaries in the whole country, and he also knew that they themselves would not deny the charge.

Certainly the sentiments expressed in their articles and speeches were highly contentious. Up till then, Mrs. Stanton asserted that woman had been the greatest unpaid labourer in the world. Taught that education for her was indelicate and irreligious, she had been kept in such ignorance as to fall a prey to superstition. Taught that a low voice is an excellent thing in woman, she had been trained to a subjugation of the vocal chords, and thus had lost the benefit of loud tones and their well-known invigoration of the system.

Forbidden to run, climb and jump, her muscles had been weakened and her strength had deteriorated. Confined most of the time to the house, she had neither as strong lungs nor as vigorous a digestion as her brother. Forbidden the medical profession, she had at the most sacred times of her life been left to the ignorant supervision of male physicians and had seen her young children die by thousands.

Forbidden to enter the courts, woman had seen her sex unjustly tried and condemned for crimes men were incapable of judging.

"The usual masculine grace has long been a thorn in my flesh," Mrs. Stanton once confided to an audience. "It is enough to make all the feminine angels weep to see a bumptious man, with a good appetite, spread his hands over a nicely roasted turkey which his little wife has basted and turned for two hours in a hot oven, and thank the Lord as if the whole meal had come down from Heaven, whereas one little pair of hands had like magic produced the whole meal. When I am called upon for a grace, here is what I say: 'Heavenly Father and Mother make us thankful for all the blessings of this life, and make us ever mindful of the patient hands that oft in weariness spread our tables and prepare our daily food. For Humanity's sake, Amen.' " It is interesting to note from this that Mrs. Stanton believed God to be equally male and female.

One afternoon in 1854, the wife of a Congressman called on her and asked for advice. The timid little woman disclosed that her kitchen stove smoked and leaked. It was a worthless thing which could neither bake nor broil, and it was too small for any purpose. Consequently half their meals were spoilt, and the cooks left in disgust, one after another.

"Then why don't you buy a new stove?" Elizabeth enquired.

"Because I have never purchased anything, not even a darning needle, without consulting my husband, and he does not think a new stove necessary."

Mrs. Stanton's eyes flashed. "What pray, does he know about stoves, sitting in his easy chair in Washington? If he had a dull old knife with broken blade, he would soon get a new one with which to sharpen his pens and pencils and, if he attempted to cook a meal— granting he knew how—on your old stove, he would set it out of doors the next hour. Now my advice to you is to buy a new one this very day!"

"Bless me! That would make him furious. He would blow me sky-high!"

"Well, suppose he did go into a regular tantrum and

use all the most startling expletives in the vocabulary for fifteen minutes, what is that compared with a good stove three hundred and sixty-five days in a year? Just put all he could say on one side, and all the advantages you would enjoy on the other, and you must readily see that his wroth would kick the beam."

"Well, Mrs. Stanton, if you'll go with me, and help me select a stove, I think I will take the responsibility."

Accordingly the two women went to the hardware store and selected the most approved, largest-sized stove, with all the best cooking utensils. "Now, is there anything else that you need while we're here?" Elizabeth asked. The other hesitated. "Well, I am in equal need of a good stove in my sitting-room. I like the look of that nickel-plated 'Morning Glory' over there. And I would like the pipes of both stoves to lead into dumb-stoves above, and thus heat two or three rooms upstairs for my children to play in, as they have no place except the sitting-room, where they must always be with me, but I suppose it is best not to do too much at one time."

"On the contrary, as your husband is wealthy, you had better get all you really need now. He will probably be no more surprised with two stoves than with one and, as you expect a hot scene over the matter, the more you get out of it the better."

So stoves and pipes were ordered, holes cut through the ceiling, and all was in working order next day. The cook was delighted with her splendid stove and shining tins, the new copper-bottomed tea-kettle and boiler, and her warm sleeping-room upstairs. The children rejoiced over their large heated playrooms, and their mother was at last able to enjoy a little peace on her own, relaxing in front of the "Morning Glory" in the sitting-room.

Fortunately her husband was away in Washington

at the time, but when his home-coming drew near, she grew nervous and called once more on Mrs. Stanton.

"Having studied the *genus homo* alike on the divine heights of exaltation and in the valleys of humiliation, I think I might be able to make some valuable suggestions."

"Oh, please do, Mrs. Stanton!"

"Now, when your husband explodes as you think he will, neither say nor do anything. Sit and gaze out of the window with that far-away, sad look women know so well how to affect. If you can summon tears at pleasure, a few would not be amiss—a gentle shower—not enough to make the nose and eyes red or to detract from your beauty. Men cannot resist beauty and tears."

"Is that so?"

"Never mar their effect with anything bordering on sobs and hysteria—such violent manifestations being neither refined nor artistic. A scene in which one person does the talking must be limited in time. No ordinary man can keep at white heat for fifteen minutes. If his victim says nothing, he will soon exhaust himself. Remember, every time you speak in the way of defence, you give him a new text on which to branch out again. If silence is ever golden, it is when a husband is in a tantrum.

"How can a man know what implements are necessary for the work he never does? Of all agencies for upsetting the equanimity of family life, none can surpass an old, broken-down kitchen stove."

The Congressman's wife went away reassured by all this, but fortunately for her the outcome of her venture was a happy one. It was a cold, icy, winter's evening when her lord and master returned covered with snow and with frozen hands and feet. The unexpected warmth of the house both upstairs and down, and the

123

wonderful dinner the happy cook had prepared on the new stove thawed him at once, and he called his wife a clever little woman for having read his thoughts and for buying the stoves and things which he, but for the cares of state, would have bought long ago.

Meek married women—spaniel wives, as she called them—were always being incited by Mrs. Stanton to stand up to their husbands. Letting off steam through vituperation was good for their health. She advised them to loosen their stays first, so as to have the fullest use of their lungs. One wonders how many found the courage to take her advice.

Not all women agreed with Mrs. Stanton. Some still clung to the belief that a woman's place was in the home. A disapproving mother at a meeting asked Mrs. Stanton: "What do you do with your children?" To which she replied: "Madam, it takes me no longer to speak than you to listen. What have you done with your children, the two hours you have been sitting here?"

Elizabeth enjoyed being heckled. She always had a ready answer, especially for the male interrupter: "The rooster may do the crowing, but the faithful hen lays the eggs."

It particularly pleased her to remind listeners that a red petticoat tied to a sailor's blue jacket and a woman's white apron was used to make the first American flag. Therefore so long as "Old Glory" flew over them, the men of the thirteen states were tied symbolically to a woman's apron strings.

She pointed out, too, that the idea of Savings Banks was originated by a woman, Mrs. Priscilla Wakefield, and suggested that women should be in charge of them. They were natural helpers and should be entrusted with the management of all charities and funds where their own sex and children were concerned. This would guard against the risk of men embezzling the funds, as had already happened.

One of Mrs. Stanton's ideas was far in advance of her own times. She advocated that young women should pay for their own amusements, instead of expecting their escorts to do so. The current fashion, she insisted, was degrading to her own sex and an unnecessary drain on a young man's pocket.

XI

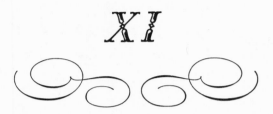

NEW WORLDS TO CONQUER

Mrs. Bloomer in after years often referred with pride to the fact that she had been responsible for introducing Miss Anthony to Mrs. Stanton. She believed that without Susan's drive, Elizabeth would never have achieved half she did. Amelia regarded her part in forging this friendship, together with the influence of her paper, as important contributions to the success of the Women's Rights Movement.

The Lily was now a widely-read, widely quoted, thriving publication, coming out twice a month and "scattering the good women's rights doctrines from Canada to Florida, and from Maine to California"— to quote Mrs. Bloomer's own words.

Few copies of *The Lily* remain in existence. Reading through its pages, one becomes conscious of the changes in outlook of its Editress—from her first tentative steps in the fields of the Women's Rights Movement to her bolder marching in the van, brave in Bloomer battle-dress. She was a great critic, but had a kind heart and a forgiving nature. If she had a fault, it was that she took life too seriously. This is perhaps most noticeable in her references to intoxicating liquors.

Amelia was appalled when in New York to discover that in the chief town of her State there were elegantly appointed parlours frequented by fashionable, wealthy women, who went there "first for ice-creams, then for claret, champagne, mint juleps, sherry cobblers, and brandy slings".

She reported the existence of these black spots to her readers and commented: "These so-called respectable ladies are in our view decidedly vulgar and should be classed in public estimation with the drunken occupant of the shanty or the frequenter of the low drunkery. They are even worse than them, for their influence is greater."

Her own favourite place for refreshment, she told readers, was Mr. Skidmore's Temperance Recess in Fall Street, which was "neatly fitted up and well supplied with refreshments that will not intoxicate. He gets up the best of soda and ice cream—than which nothing can be more acceptable this hot weather."

All temperance novels could be certain of favourable reviews in *The Lily,* and as a result the publishers of such literature regularly bought advertising space, offering occasionally such bargains as "Mr. Sargent's Temperance Tales, all 21 for one dollar; special price in lots of one hundred."

She was very particular about what advertisements she accepted. To a tobacco grower who wished to advertise in her Christmas issue she wrote: "Tobacco is a fruitful cause of drunkenness. That it creates a thirst is admitted by those who use it. Consequently the more a man smokes the more he drinks. I will not advertise poisons in my paper."

Very occasionally, Mrs. Bloomer would publish a

contribution written by a male. During the paper's first year, it ran a series of articles upon the Nebular Theory from the pen of the local druggist, Mr. Mattson. However, it did not prove popular with her readers, so she never repeated the experiment.

She was an adept at thinking up space fillers, such as "Sweep carpets as seldom as possible; it takes off the wool and leaves the thread bare, injuring its beauty and texture." Then again: "Old Maid—a lady who has attained the age of twenty-five without having married a fool, a gambler, a knave, or a drunkard". Or this warning to shoppers: "Be careful what candles you buy. Some shops are selling hollow ones containing fourth-proof brandy and low-grade rum."

Whenever a temperance or women's rights convention was held anywhere in the States, Mrs. Bloomer would do her best to attend and make a speech. If her work at the Post Office prevented her from doing so, she would write a letter to the lady chairman to be read at the meeting and also publish it later in *The Lily*.

Dexter, her husband, was tiring of his work as Postmaster. He regretted that he was no longer part editor and owner of *The Courier*. Many a time he had confided to Amelia how he wished he could go back once more into active journalism. The opportunity provided itself in the spring of 1853 when he accompanied his wife to a women's rights convention in Cleveland, Ohio. They went on afterwards to visit Mount Vernon, which was a pleasant town of about six thousand inhabitants. Whilst there Dexter learnt that the local paper, the *Western Home Visitor,* needed capital for expansion. He approached the owner and editor, Mr. E. A. Higgins. The two men liked each other from the start and it was agreed that they should become partners.

This meant, of course, that the Bloomers would have

Scene from the fairy burlesque of the "Princess Radiant" at the Haymarket Theatre, December 1851.

A probable result next Derby Day. Drawing by J. Leech from "The Month—A View of Passing Subjects and Manners."

Susan B. Anthony.

Lucy Stone.

PARIS FASHIONS FOR APRIL.

Victoria & Albert Museum.

Fashions for 1865.

"AN EASTER OFFERING."

Punch Cartoon.

The Cage Crinoline.

Mr. and Mrs. Bloomer in Old Age.

Council Bl

Looking North.

Mrs. Oscar Wilde.

A Regular Scorcher

The New Sport for Ladies.

Cycling Fa

1890s.

Radio Times Hulton Picture Library.

"Ready for a Spin." 1895.

Madame du Gast wearing a divided skirt in the 1890s.

Bloomer Costume in 1967.

to leave Seneca Falls. The December issue of *The Lily* gave news of this to its readers. Amelia wrote: "Our husband, having purchased an interest in the *Western Home Visitor* published at Mount Vernon, Ohio, and determined on moving to that place forthwith, we, as a true and faithful wife, are bound to say in the language of Ruth 'where thou goest I will go', and so, before another number of *The Lily* reaches its subscribers, we shall, if all is well, be settled in our western home."

Mrs. Bloomer went on to say that all this might be an unpleasant surprise to many of her readers and friends. She hoped that they would not cease taking the paper as a result. It would continue to be published as formerly and its character would be in no way changed. " 'Uncle Sam' will carry it as safely and regularly to your homes as he has hitherto, and will also carry all letters and remittances to us as safely and securely in Ohio as in New York. Then, friends, we pray you let not our change of location affect our intercourse with each other."

The departure of the Bloomers caused much regret in Seneca Falls. To her delight, her old opponent Mr. Isaac Fuller, the editor of the *Seneca County Courier*, published the following in the next issue of his paper: "Although we disapprove of some of the measures advocated in *The Lily,* we part with it and its worthy editor with regret. It is now five years since its publication was commenced, and during the whole time Mrs. Bloomer has had the entire direction of it both editorially and financially, displaying talents and business qualifications possessed by few of the gentler sex and which but few of her friends were prepared to see her exhibit. The ability and energy with which *The Lily* has been conducted have attained for it a circulation of over four thousand copies in different parts of the Union, thus giving to our enterprising village notoriety which it would not have otherwise obtained."

Mr. Fuller went on to say that he had heard strangers who had never met the Editress of *The Lily* describe her as "a coarse, unrefined woman, possessing few or none of the traits which adorn the female character, and as cherishing a disregard of the duties devolving upon woman in the domestic relations of society". He assured the world at large that just the reverse was the truth.

He ended by hoping that *The Lily* would lose none of its vitality through being transplanted, and that "its amiable editor would enjoy a long and happy life".

So popular were the Bloomers that some five hundred people of all classes, half of them women, attended a farewell party held one Tuesday evening in the Union Hall.

After the refreshments were disposed of, speeches were made to which Dexter and Amelia replied. Then came music and dancing, which festivities, Amelia tells us, were prolonged to a late hour.

The *Western Home Visitor* was a weekly paper with a large circulation. It had progressive tendencies, advocated temperance and sound morality, and published nothing which could not be read by the whole family. It accepted no advertisements and depended entirely on its readers' yearly subscriptions.

Amelia became its Assistant Editor. Her very first article read: "Salutatory! Following the custom set to me by my husband, I make my editorial bow to the readers of the *Visitor*. I suppose it is not necessary for me to enter into any detailed account of myself, as the papers have already done that for me. Neither do I suppose it necessary to make any statement in regard to my sentiments and principles as they are already generally well-known to the public. What I have been in the past, I expect to be in the future—an uncompromising opponent of wrong and oppression in every form, and a sustainer of the right and the true, with whatever subject it may be connected."

Her next article was headed "Woman's Right to Employment". In this she claimed that all women should be engaged in some active useful employment and that, if this were denied them, they became enfeebled in health and prematurely old. She rejected the idea that it was not respectable for a woman to earn her own living. Parents were to be censured who kept their daughters at home in inactivity and indolence.

It had been said by a distinguished clergyman of a lady who had passed from this earth: "She ate, she drank, she slept, she dressed, she danced, and she died." Such might truly be said to be the history of so many women of that time. But a great change was on the way.

Meanwhile *The Lily* thrived in its new environment. She changed its form from folio to quarto, and had it printed in new type on a steam press. Everyone thought it looked very neat and handsome. New subscriptions poured in and its circulation rose to over six thousand.

During the year she spent in Ohio, Amelia received a great many invitations asking her to lecture to various societies. In one town in Indiana she was invited to speak to a young men's literary society. No fee had been fixed in advance. She did not expect to be paid much, but on being told that she had attracted a larger audience and brought in more money than any other lecturer, even the famous Horace Mann, who had spoken at the previous month's meeting, she said to the treasurer: "You say I have done better for you than

Horace Mann, then pay me what you paid him and it will be all right." She thought he seemed a little surprised that a woman should ask as much as a man, but seeing the justice of her demand, he paid her without a word.

One day, it occurred to her that she should do something practical herself in the way of opening up new forms of employment to her sex. She discussed the matter with Dexter, and with his agreement engaged early in the spring of 1853 Mrs. C. W. Lundy of New York as a typesetter. She had had three months' previous experience.

The other employees were all men, who were told about Mrs. Lundy's recruitment before she arrived. No word of disapproval was uttered in Dexter's presence. It was arranged that she should receive personal training from Mr. Higgins himself, and from the men engaged in the office. It was soon apparent, however, that the typesetters, and in particular their foreman, were hostile to the experiment. They were openly rude to her and did everything they could to make her give up the job.

The men's attitude did not come to the notice of Mrs. Bloomer till one day when both her husband and Mr. Higgins were away on business and Mrs. Lundy came into Amelia's office to ask her opinion regarding the correct indentation of a piece of poetry she was trying to set. She apologized for doing so, explaining that none of the men would help her in any way.

The Editress of *The Lily* immediately went into the typesetters' room and asked the foreman for an explanation. He told her that the men had authorized him to say that they refused to go on working any longer with a woman, and that either Mrs. Lundy must be dismissed at once or they would walk out. He handed Mrs.

Bloomer a written statement to that effect, which had been signed not only by them but by all the male type-setters in Mount Vernon. The foreman defied her to find a printer anywhere in Ohio who would give instructions to a woman.

That evening, Amelia discussed the situation with Dexter and Mr. Higgins and the two men agreed that whatever the cost Mrs. Lundy would not be dismissed. Next day, they addressed a meeting of the malcontents, making it clear that it was not the intention to employ women to set the type of the *Visitor,* and pointing out that Mrs. Lundy had been employed to work on *The Lily* and that she would continue in that capacity. The men were told that it was expected that they should give her in future all the assistance she might need in her work. If they would agree to do this, willingly and cheerfully, this rebellion would be forgotten; but, if they would not co-operate, they might consider them-selves dismissed.

The typesetters refused to retreat from their stand and marched out. The Bloomers at once engaged three women who soon became expert typesetters under Mr. Higgins' personal instruction. Two male hands were in due course engaged to help them. Amelia had the cases for *The Lily* moved into the same room that housed those of the *Visitor.* The four women and the three men worked together peaceably and har-moniously. Mrs. Bloomer wrote to a friend that it did her heart good to see the happy change which had been wrought in the office by the attempt to get rid of Mrs. Lundy. "The moral atmosphere has been purified, and superciliousness has given place to friendly and cheerful intercourse."

The case of Mrs. Lundy caused quite a stir in Mount Vernon. In the midst of all the controversy thus aroused amongst the citizens, Miss Lucy Stone came to the town and most appropriately gave a lecture on "Woman and her Employment".

"It seemed as though benign providence had directed her to step hitherwards to allay the excitement and to subdue the angry feelings," wrote Amelia. This timely visit helped to bring round public opinion in favour of her stand against the strikers.

During the summer of 1853, she went back on a visit to Seneca Falls and was warmly welcomed by all her old friends. Whilst there she attended the annual general meeting of the Women's State Temperance Society in New York. A resolution was proposed that as the best physicians of the day had agreed that smoking was injurious to health, steps should be taken to prevent young people from becoming addicts. Mrs. Bloomer spoke in favour of the proposals. She blamed the parents for not setting an example. They seemed to think that it was only natural for their sons to take up smoking. "In consequence, one sees little fellows who have hardly escaped from their frocks, smoking the cigar or long pipe in perfect imitation of their elders and this, too, without reproach or warning from those who should teach them better. The practice, if continued will prove ruinous to health, if no more terrible results follow." Grimly prophetic words.

The western half of the United States in those days was undeveloped country, but it was gradually being opened up. Mrs. Bloomer had on more than one occasion urged her readers in *The Lily* to persuade their husbands and sons to go out West. Whenever she saw a stout and athletic man standing behind a counter measuring lace, ribbons and tape, she felt that he was monopolizing woman's place, whilst thousands of rich acres in the western world awaited his coming.

Dexter Bloomer had for long shared his wife's views in this matter and whilst she was away from home he set out on his own, going as far as western Iowa and Nebraska. He was very taken with the small town of Council Bluffs, which lies in the centre of the United States, three miles east of the Missouri river. It had received its name from the council held there in 1804 by the explorers, Meriwether Lewis and William Clark, with the Indians. In 1838, the Federal Government had made it the headquarters for the Pottawattamie Indians, who had been removed from Missouri. They left in 1846 with the arrival of the Mormons, who in their turn departed some six years later for Utah. They were swiftly replaced by immigrants from the east coast. The gold rush of 1849 gave it great importance, for it was here that those seeking gold in California were able to buy their outfits, easily conveyed along the river from St. Louis.

When Dexter reached Council Bluffs for the first time, its population was just over two thousand. There were no sidewalks and nearly all the buildings were built of logs. Land was being sold at the local Government office at $1.25 an acre—the equivalent of five shillings at the then current rate of exchange. With his lawyer's mind, he realized the possibilities of this growing town with its rich, fertile soil and fine natural position. The level lands between it and the river were well drained and in no danger of being flooded. Beyond them ran a chain of high hills or bluffs, which lined the Missouri for thousands of miles, and which at that point extended eastwards some five or six miles.

These bluffs were composed of immense piles of yellow marl, varying in height from fifty to two hundred feet, and thrown into every conceivable shape and form —rounded, oblong, conical and peaked. Here and there,

135

they were covered with trees and bushes but mostly with only grass and flowers.

How Amelia would love this place, thought Dexter, as he looked down from the heights at the beautiful valleys between the bluffs through which clear streams of water flowed gurgling down to join the mighty Missouri, streams which glistened like silver in the sun. The bracing air, too, he felt would be good for his wife's health. Here she could gain that much needed rest which years of labour and activity had rendered necessary.

He bought some land in a position where there was nothing to obstruct the view and, after arranging for a log house to be built, returned to Mount Vernon to tell Amelia what he had done.

As he expected, she thoroughly approved of his action. Now at last, she was going to do what she had advised others to do—go pioneering in the West. There was only one drawback to the move. Council Bluffs was three hundred miles beyond the railroad, and there were no facilities for printing and mailing a paper with so large a circulation as *The Lily* except a handpress and a stage-coach. So, reluctantly, she decided it would be best for her to part with the paper.

Fortunately it had such a reputation that she had no difficulty in finding a purchaser in Mrs. Mary A. Birdsall of Richmond, Indiana, and she travelled there to hand over in person all that went with *The Lily*—type, cases, subscription list and past files. While in the town she took the opportunity to give a lecture on women's wrongs and rights. She also promised Mrs. Birdsall that she would continue to write for the paper, a promise she kept for as long as the paper existed.

Whilst Dexter arranged his affairs and disposed of his interests in Mount Vernon, Amelia spent the next

136

few months visiting all her relatives and friends in New York State. They waited for the winter to end before embarking on the fifteen hundred mile journey to Council Bluffs on March 20th, 1855.

They travelled in stages. Their first stop was at Little Rock near Buffalo where they stayed a few days with Dexter's brother; then they continued to Chicago, where Amelia received a heart-warming reception from Mr. F. V. Chamberlain, her former pupil of long ago, now married and with a family of his own. The Chamberlains insisted on their now famous friend and her husband spending several days in their home.

From Chicago they went by railroad through unbroken prairies, with deer and other game roaming at large, until they reached the terminus at Alton, Illinois, on the Mississippi. Here they continued their journey by steamboat to St. Louis where, after staying a few days with her old friend, the feminist poet Mrs. Frances Gage, they embarked on another steamer, hoping that it would take them straight to their final destination. Unfortunately they could get no further than St. Joseph, owing to the low water in the Missouri.

"Here we had to wait two days for the stage which only made tri-weekly trips to Council Bluffs and had left the very morning of our coming, some hours before we arrived. The hotel at which we were obliged to stop was a very ordinary affair, as was common to western towns at that early day. The waiting was long and tedious. We could not even walk about and view the city because of a high wind that sent the dust in clouds into our faces." Thus wrote Amelia in her diary.

On the second day, two men called at the hotel and presented a petition, signed by the leading citizens of the town, asking her to give a lecture on women's rights before she left. Amelia told them that this was impossible, for she was leaving that very evening by the ten o'clock stage.

The men replied that they knew this, and wanted her to speak that evening before she left. Amelia asked how they expected to assemble an audience in so short a time.

"It is a little after seven o'clock," said one of her visitors, consulting his watch. "We will give you a good house in an hour, if you will consent to speak—the lecture to commence at eight p.m." His companion nodded agreement.

Amelia reluctantly consented. She had many misgivings, for she could not believe that they could assemble an audience in an hour. But she had made it a rule never to turn down an invitation to propagate the new doctrine of women's rights, when she found people anxious to hear her message.

Amelia ran up to her bedroom to tell Dexter what she had agreed to do. Their trunk was already packed and strapped and had to be opened so that she could change. While she was doing this, they were startled to hear a great outcry and ringing of bells in the street.

"Rushing to the window, we saw passing along the sidewalk below a large black man ringing a dinner bell. Every other minute the bell would stop, and then came forth the stentorian cry: "Mrs. Bloomer will lecture at the Courthouse at eight o'clock tonight!" Then the bell again, and again the cry; and the same cry and ringing of bells off in the other streets, till the town was alive with noise. We were greatly amused over this novel western way of giving a notice and calling a crowd together, and we realized then how fully a notice could be given in the time fixed."

Mrs. Bloomer found the Courthouse filled with an eager and curious crowd that had come to see and listen to the strange woman "whose name and doings had startled the world from its old time peace and sobriety". It was the first time one of the "women agitators" had come so far west as St. Joseph, so it was not strange that an apprehensive audience awaited her.

Her success can be gauged from the fact that hardly had she returned to her hotel before the two men who had arranged the meeting came hurrying into the parlour begging her to stay on at St. Joseph and give a series of lectures, and promising to make it financially worth her while.

But Mrs. Bloomer refused, for she had given her lecture despite a severe cold and was anxious to reach her journey's end. The stage was late, and it was not until two o'clock on a rainy morning that they at last set forth. She was the only woman passenger. Her companions consisted of several young male emigrants and the famous Kit Carson, the hunter and scout, then in his forty-seventh year, who was returning to his home. Having heard much of him, she eyed him with curiosity. "But I saw nothing remarkable about him, except his clothes which were of buckskin, fringed around the bottom, wrists and collar, a style entirely new to me."

One of the young men came from Massachusetts and was going to Nebraska to seek his fortune. Unfortunately, he had run out of money. At one of the stages where they changed horses, he approached Mr. Bloomer and asked him for a loan. As Dexter did not know him, he gave him the money he wanted, but took his watch as security. However, when the time came for the lad to leave them, Dexter returned him the watch. A few months later, this act of trust was justified when the borrower repaid his debt.

By the time they crossed a ferry into Nebraska, they

were the only passengers. Amelia found it a relief to be alone with Dexter in the coach after riding two days and a night crowded together with eight men. It was spring time and the country through which they passed was beautiful. She was enchanted with all they saw, and felt that they were indeed coming to a land of promise.

At about five o'clock on the afternoon of April 15th, 1855, the stage-coach reached Council Bluffs.

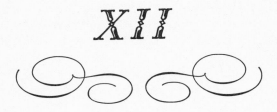

XII

COUNCIL BLUFFS

THEY STAYED at first in what was then *the* hotel of Council Bluffs, the Pacific Hotel. It was primitive accommodation compared with East Coast standards, but Amelia had already prepared herself to lead the life of a pioneer for the next few years and put up with all inconveniences without complaint.

They remained in the hotel for two weeks, hoping in vain that a rise in the river would float a boat bringing their household goods up from St. Louis. But they grew tired of inaction and when a kind friend offered to lend them some furniture and bedding, they gladly accepted the offer and moved into their newly built house in Bancroft Street. Years later it was to be renamed Fourth Street and their residence was to become "No. 123", but in 1855 all the road contained, apart from the Bloomers' abode, was a frame house on one side and a log house on the other.

Their own log house was covered on the outside with cottonwood boards, whilst on the inside walls and ceilings were lined with unbleached muslin sewn together and nailed on. They occupied only two rooms whilst they waited for their own things to arrive. In these rough quarters they had two old wooden chairs, an old table, three trunks and a bed made on the floor. They had been lent two bedsteads, but they were useless as they could not find the screws.

"To these borrowed things, we added an old-fashioned stove that we were fortunate to find here, and a few common dishes," wrote Amelia in her diary. "Here, with these surroundings, I received my first calls, and made my first acquaintances. If more than two happened to call at the same time, the two chairs were utilized as far as they would go, and I and the others sat on the trunks. We made the best of it, knowing it was not for good."

Amelia was glad to find that her odd furniture and surroundings made no difference to the warmth of her welcome from Council Bluffs' society. Later, she discovered that many others were little better off, for there were no furniture or carpet stores in the city.

In May, she wrote to her friend, Mrs. Vaughan, in Seneca Falls. "The business of housekeeping, as you will know, is not new to me, but it is a long time since I have confined myself to that business alone, and it seems a little strange, after the many and various duties devolved upon me for the last six or seven years, to be relieved of the greater part of them, and to settle down in a strange place with nothing to care for, save my house and garden."

She went on to say how she loved to ascend the bluffs at the rear of her house and watch the setting sun. "As I do so, I contemplate the day when the wild valley below me will be filled with the hum and stir of a great city, and these bluffs covered with elegant residences

142

and tasteful retreats from the turmoil and activity that will reign below."

In another letter to the same friend she described the situation of her own house as being on a gentle elevation at the foot of one of the highest bluffs in the city. From her front door she had a fine view, first of the grass-carpeted bottoms upon which hundreds of cattle were grazing, then of the city of Omaha on the other side of the river, beyond which stretched the plains of Nebraska as far as the eye could see.

She assured Mrs. Vaughan that she was not surrounded by hordes of savage Indians and in danger of falling a victim to the tomahawk and scalping knife, as some people in the East imagined. The Indians she had encountered were perfectly harmless and she liked them. A party of Pawnees had recently pitched their tents on the summit of a high bluff near her house and had been there for a fortnight. She wished she could speak their language for it had distressed her to see the men riding on horseback when they left, while the squaws went on foot with papooses on their backs. One squaw had carried a dog in the same manner. "I was very interested in these children of nature and I almost regretted their departure."

Later she wrote that they would be seeing little of any Red Indians in the future, as the Government had just paid off its indebtedness to the Omahas, and were removing them all to the new reservations assigned them a hundred miles to the north.

"They were all collected at Omaha City, and from thence started on their journey, accompanied by the Indian agent who was to pay them twenty thousand dollars in cash, when they reached their destination. The tribe now numbers eight hundred and five, counting men, women and children, and has but two hundred men capable of bearing arms. Ten years ago they numbered sixteen hundred. Their parting from their old home and the graves of their fathers is said by those who witnessed it to have been exceedingly pathetic. The women and the aged men wept, and even the stout-hearted warriors could ill-conceal their emotion."

It was not till the morning of the fourth of July that a steamer arrived with the Bloomers' household goods. Amelia was delighted to be able to put down her carpets at last, and concentrate on making her little home pleasant and inviting. She spent her few leisure hours going for long walks over the bluffs and through the valleys.

There were only two churches in the town, one Methodist and the other Congregationalist. Although the Bloomers had become Episcopalians soon after their marriage, they were broad-minded and, so long as they could worship somewhere on Sundays, were willing to attend any Christian church. When the Congregationalist minister called on her and offered to allow her to lecture from his pulpit on female education, she accepted, and became one of his congregation.

These talks were so successful that she was invited by the Men's Literary and Debating Society to speak on women's emancipation in the Methodist church, where she made such an impression that she was approached after the meeting by General Larimer, a member of the first Nebraska Legislature, who asked whether she would be willing to go to Omaha and repeat her speech before the House of Representatives. She agreed to do so and a few days later a formal invitation, signed by twenty-five members, was sent to her.

On January 8th, 1856, Mrs. Bloomer made her appearance in the House of Representatives. Men

144

stood between those who were sitting and others leant against the walls. General Larimer escorted her to the platform, so crowded right up to the desk from which Amelia spoke, that she hardly had elbow room.

The General introduced her to the Assembly. She pleaded the cause of Woman's Suffrage with such cogent arguments and eloquence that there was complete silence for a moment when she sat down. Then came shouts of approval and thunderous applause. There was no doubt about it, she had scored a personal triumph.

The papers all published flattering reports and as a result a bill was brought in a few days later in favour of giving women the vote in the State of Nebraska. It passed the lower house with a large majority, was read twice by the Senate, and only failed to be approved by the latter because the session came to an end before it could be reached for a third reading.

Amelia became the most talked about and sought after person in the State. The Library Association of Omaha invited her to give them a lecture on education for women, which she agreed to do. It was a bitter winter's evening when she left her home; the river was frozen and people had been crossing it on foot. But when she reached the banks she found that the ice had started to break up. On the other side, she could see the carriage waiting to take her to the hall in Omaha. To attempt the crossing on foot was impossible. She approached some boatmen. Could they help her in any way? They might be able to pole her over in a flat boat, two of them suggested doubtfully, but it would be a dangerous and hazardous undertaking. Amelia thought of the many people who had come out of their warm homes into the wintry weather to attend her meeting. She could not disappoint them. So she ventured on board a flat boat, telling herself that if she were drowned, it would at least be as a martyr to the women's cause. Her luck held, and she landed safely on the other side.

But if she had taken a risk going, the peril was worse returning. A high wind was blowing and when she reached the river, she found that it had broken up into great blocks of ice. The flat boat in which she had travelled over could not be managed by the boatmen in such a gale. They told her they might be able to row her back in a skiff, but that it would be in great danger of being swamped by the high waves or struck by the huge cakes of floating ice and capsized.

Some other boatmen shouted that it would be madness to take a woman on board. She was certain to get frightened, jump about, rock the boat and perhaps even capsize it. But Mrs. Bloomer pleaded with them, promising to sit very still and not stir. "A gentleman intervened and, on my promise, I was allowed to get into the boat. I sat in the middle of my seat and held on to each side. I am sure I never stirred a muscle or winked an eye or hardly breathed, while those brave men guided their skiff over the tossing waves, which seemed to engulf us at times and anon bore us on their crests. But soon we were safely over and landed, and ready to take stage for home."

When Mrs. Bloomer first came to Council Bluffs, she continued wearing the Bloomer costume as her working dress, and donned long skirts when she lectured or went to parties. Unfortunately for her, however, she found that the high winds which prevailed in that part of the world much of the time, played tricks with her short skirt when she went out. She was greatly annoyed and mortified by having her skirt turned over her head and shoulders in the main street. Despite this, she perse-

146

vered and partially solved the problem by weighting the hem of her skirt with shot. It was not altogether satisfactory, for the winds lashed her legs with the weighted skirt, bruising them.

In Paris, a new fashion had been launched which enabled a woman to dispense with all her petticoats. This was the artificial crinoline. It consisted of graduated wire hoops, held together by narrow strips of material. Later it was improved by using watch-spring instead of wire.

Never did a fashion spread more quickly, and the inventor of this 'bird cage' is said to have made a profit of half a million francs in a month. Mrs. Bloomer tried one on at the house of an acquaintance who had been sent the crinoline as a Christmas present by her sister who lived in New York. Amelia has recorded her reactions in one of her notebooks.

"Finding the hoops light and pleasant to wear, and doing away with the necessity for heavy underclothes (which was my greatest objection to long dresses) and finding it very inconvenient as well as expensive keeping two wardrobes—a long and a short—I gradually left off wearing the short dress.

"I consulted my own feelings and inclinations and judgment in laying it off, believing that I had the same right to doff that I had to don it, and not expecting to be accountable for my doings and required to give a reason to everyone that asked me. There were other questions of greater importance than the length of a skirt under discussion at the time, and I felt my influence would be greater in the dress ordinarily worn by women than in the one I was wearing."

Amelia had worn a dress when she had addressed the Nebraska Legislature, with the aim of making herself as appealingly feminine as possible and to win over her male audience. It had proved a most successful experiment. After all, she had never intended to be first and foremost a dress reformer, but the Bloomer costume had been a useful device to give the feminist movement world-wide publicity. Having achieved that, her main purpose now was to help fashion the way of life for this new State and to influence the making of its laws so that women could obtain there the rights they were still denied in the older States.

She foresaw a tremendous future for Council Bluffs. It was three hundred miles west of the railroads, connecting the Mississippi with the cities of the East. In an article in *The Lily* urging its readers to consider seriously the advantages of emigrating to the Middle West, she wrote: "We, of course, neither hear the shrill whistle of the locomotive nor see the train of cars dashing through our streets with a velocity that outstrips the speed of the light foot deer—but we are living in full expectation of the day when these things will be as familiar to us as they now are to my eastern readers. This city will one day be the western terminus of the first railroad built across the States, and it is fondly hoped and expected that three years hence we shall be startled by the shrill whistle of the iron horse, as he comes to bathe his head in the waters of the Missouri; and from here, or from Omaha, directly opposite, will he set out on his long journey to the most western limit of the continent. Then Council Bluffs will no longer be out of the world but directly in the centre of it, and many who now hesitate about making their home here will regret that their doubts and fears debarred them from uniting their labour with their more enterprising countrymen in building up a great and prosperous community." She wrote this in 1855. She was remarkably correct in prophesying a fine future for Council Bluffs, although it took nearly ten years instead of three before the railroad reached it.

Already they were starting to build brick buildings as fast as materials and labour could be obtained. On all sides, the work of improving the town was going forward. "Gardens were being fenced, trees planted and the beaten paths through the fields of sunflowers that once answered for thoroughfares, were being made into roads."

By the following year, people were beginning to flock there in considerable numbers, either to settle or to make investments in real estate in the hope of reaping a fortune by the rise in value of property.

Owing largely to Amelia's endeavours, laws were passed allowing women to own and hold property, both real and personal. She was happy to find that many women availed themselves of the opportunity to become landowners. She wrote to her friend, Mrs. Vaughan, that she was especially anxious that she and those women "who labour so untiringly with you in the cause of humanity should come in for a share".

She knew that such women were not usually very well off as women were so ill-paid for their work. Yet with land as cheap as $1.25 per acre, she thought that most of them ought to be able to buy at least eighty acres. It would be worth ten times its cost within a year, she assured her. She mentioned that one of the women type-setters from Mount Vernon had already bought a hundred acres, and was hoarding her wages so that she might each month add a few more acres to those she had already acquired.

She begged Mrs. Vaughan and all her other friends not to procrastinate. "Make up your minds and come quickly," she wrote. "Stages are now being run daily from the East and South and they generally come loaded, inside and out, to the extent of their capacity. The Government Land Office is crowded all day by settlers and speculators eager to purchase the choicest land remaining unsold."

Two years later all the land directly adjoining the town and for six miles outwards had all been disposed of by the Government. Good land was being resold at ten dollars per acre.

There were few reputable lawyers in the town and Dexter C. Bloomer had more work than he could cope with, inspecting title deeds, preparing conveyances and the like. He became the most respected man in the town. The idea of starting up a paper occurred to him, but he felt he would be doing more useful work for the community by guarding it from sharks and scoundrels.

And thus, "far from the place of my birth," as Amelia wrote in her diary, "far from the noble spirits with whom I have long laboured in the cause of humanity, far from all I have best known and loved, save him who is my companion in life's journey," she commenced life anew, doing what she could by her aid and influence for the upbringing and prosperity of the infant city of Council Bluffs.

XIII

CAMPAIGNING IN KANSAS

THE EXAMPLE set by Mrs. Bloomer in going pioneering in the rugged West encouraged other feminists to do the same. Mrs. Stanton and Miss Anthony were foremost in this respect, embarking on long and arduous propaganda tours in all weathers. Council Bluffs was certain to be a halting-place on these trips, for they knew that Amelia would go to the greatest trouble to make them comfortable, happy guests in her home.

One night, when crossing the Mississippi at McGregor, Iowa, on such a tour, Elizabeth and Susan were ice-bound in the middle of the river. The boat was crowded with people; hungry, tired and cross with the delay. Some men with whom they had been talking, started the cry, "Speech on woman suffrage!"

"Accordingly, in the middle of the river, at midnight," recorded Mrs. Stanton, "we presented our claims to political representation, and debated the question of universal suffrage until we landed. Our voyagers were quite thankful that we had shortened the many hours, and we equally so at having made several converts, and having held a convention on the very bosom of the great 'Mother of Waters'."

One of the male travellers asked Miss Anthony why she had never married. She playfully replied that she could not consent that the man she loved, described by the constitution as a white male, native born American citizen, possessed of the right of self government, eligible to the office of President of the great Republic, should unite his destinies in marriage with a political slave and pariah.

Only once on this tour was Miss Anthony taken by surprise; when asked to speak to the inmates of an asylum. "Bless me!" she retorted. "It is as much as I can do to talk to the sane! What could I say to an audience of lunatics?" Her companion replied, "This is a golden moment for you, the first opportunity you have ever had, according to the constitution, to talk to your peers, for is not the right of suffrage denied to 'idiots, criminals, lunatics and women'?"

In 1867, the question as to whether the suffrage should be extended to women and coloured men was put to the vote of the people of the State of Kansas— the State to the south of Nebraska. All the leading feminists went West to take part in the campaign. Ill-health prevented Mrs. Bloomer from speaking herself in Kansas, but she made up for this with the hospitality she lavished on the women campaigners as they passed through Council Bluffs.

As there were no railroads in Kansas, the women were obliged to use carriages and to economize their forces by taking different routes. Mrs. Stanton's escort was ex-Governor Charles Robinson. They had a low-slung carriage drawn by two mules, in which they stored

about a bushel of leaflets, two valises, a pail for water-
ing the mules, a basket of apples, crackers, and such
other refreshment as they could purchase on the way.
It required great skill to compress all this into the
allotted space.

They went to the very verge of civilization, wherever
two dozen or so voters could be assembled. They spoke
in log cabins, in depots, in unfinished schools, churches,
hotels, barns and in the open. One night Mrs. Stanton
addressed the workers in a large mill. "A solitary tallow
candle shone over my head like a halo."

For three months Mrs. Stanton worked day after
day, enduring all manner of discomforts. "In going
through canyons and fording streams, it was often so
dark that the Governor was obliged to walk on ahead
to find the way, taking off his coat so that I could see
his white shirt and slowly drive after him. The Governor
often complimented me on my courage, when I was
fully aware of being tempest-tossed with anxiety. I am
naturally very timid, but being silent under strong emo-
tions of either pleasure or pain, I am credited with being
courageous in the hour of danger.

"For days, sometimes, we could find nothing at a
public table that we could eat. Then passing through a
little settlement we could buy dried herring, crackers,
gum arabic, and slippery elm; the latter, we were told
was very nutritious.... Our nights were miserable,
owing to the general opinion among pioneers that a
certain species of insect must necessarily perambulate
the beds in a young civilization.

"One night after travelling over prairies all day, eat-
ing nothing but what our larder provided, we saw a
light in a cottage in the distance which seemed to
beckon us. Arriving, we asked the usual question—if we

could get a night's lodging—to which the response was inevitably a hearty, hospitable 'Yes'. One survey of the premises showed me what to look for in the way of midnight companionship, so I said to the Governor: 'I will resign in your favour the comforts provided for me tonight, and sleep in the carriage as you do so often.' In due time, I was ensconced for the night, and all about the house was silent.

"I had just fallen into a gentle slumber, when a chorus of pronounced grunts and a spasmodic shaking of the carriage revealed to me the fact that I was surrounded by those long-nosed black pigs, so celebrated for their courage and pertinacity. They had discovered that the iron steps of the carriage made most satisfactory scratching posts, and each one was struggling for his turn.

"This scratching suggested fleas. Alas, thought I, before morning I shall be devoured. I was mortally tired and sleepy, but I reached for the whip and plied it lazily from side to side; but I soon found that nothing but a constant and most vigorous application of the whip could hold them at bay for longer than one moment.

"I had heard that this type of pig was very combative when thwarted in its desires, and they seemed in such sore need of relief that I thought there was danger of their jumping into the carriage and attacking me. This thought was more terrifying than that of the fleas, so I decided to go to sleep and let them alone to scratch at their pleasure.

"After one of these border meetings, we stopped another night with a family of two bachelor brothers and two spinster sisters. The home consisted of one large room, not yet lathed and plastered. The furniture in-

154

cluded a cooking stove, two double beds in remote corners, a table, a bureau, a washstand and six wooden chairs. As it was late, there was no fire in the stove and no suggestion of supper, so the Governor and I ate apples and chewed slippery elm before retiring to dream of well-spread tables and comfortable beds in the near future.

"The brothers resigned their bed to me just as it was. I had noticed there was no ceremonious changing of bed linen under such circumstances. When the time came for retiring, the Governor and the brothers went out to make astronomical observations or smoke as the case might be, while the sisters and I made our evening toilet, and disposed ourselves in the allotted corners. That done, the stalwart sons of Adam made their beds with skins and blankets on the floor.

"When all was still and darkness reigned, I reviewed the situation with a heavy heart, seeing that I was bound to remain a prisoner in that corner come what might. I had just congratulated myself on my powers of adaptability to circumstances, when I suddenly started with an emphatic, 'What is that?' A voice in the corner asked: 'Is your bed comfortable?' 'Oh, yes,' I replied, 'but I thought I felt a mouse run over my head.' 'Well,' said the voice in the corner, 'I should not wonder. I have heard such squeaking from that corner during the past week that I told my sister there must be a mouse nest in that bed.' A confession she probably would not have made unless half asleep. . . .

"Alas, what a prospect—to have mice running over one all night. But there was no escape. I could not lie on the floor, and the other bed was occupied. Fortunately, I was very tired and soon fell asleep. What the mice did the remainder of the night, I never knew, but as my features were intact, and my facial expression as benign as usual next morning, I inferred that their gambols had been most innocently and decorously conducted. These are samples of many similar experiences which we encountered during the three months of those eventful travels."

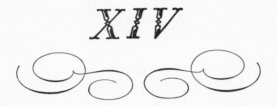

A MATCH FOR THE SENATOR

ONE OF Amelia's ambitions which she never realized was to see her sex given the vote in her home
state of Iowa. When after a long struggle, a
woman's suffrage bill was brought before the House of
Representatives in Des Moines, she travelled there, and
although on this occasion she was not invited to speak in
the State Capitol, she approached as many of the legislators as she could, putting over the case for women with
expert persuasion. Unfortunately, she had a formidable
adversary in Senator Gaylord. When put down on
paper, the arguments he advanced in his attack on the
bill were unconvincing and weak, but he was a practised
orator with every trick at his command, and he almost
hypnotized his listeners into rejecting the bill.

There was nothing Mrs. Bloomer could do, but before
returning to Council Bluffs, she sat down in her hotel
and wrote a letter to the *Des Moines Reporter* in which
she attacked and ridiculed the reasons Senator Gaylord
had given in his speech for not enfranchizing women.

"A female ought not to be compelled by law to work

out a poll-tax on the public highway," had argued the Senator, "nor to learn the art of butchery on the battle field." He claimed that if women received the vote, then it was only right that they should become liable to perform the same civic duties as men.

Mrs. Bloomer thought such reasoning absurd. Why couldn't a woman hire a substitute to do these things, just as the Senator himself did? "I venture the assertion, without knowing, that he did not earn his rights to the ballot by the bullet or by shovelling dirt on the highway. If only those who do these things were allowed to vote, the number of voters would be small indeed."

Gaylord had also claimed there was no evidence that "the most intelligent women want the miserable privilege of becoming politicians".

Amelia's comment on this was to ask if the Senator thought it a miserable privilege to have the right to vote, the right to sit in the Legislature making wise and just laws for the government of his country? A man who prized these privileges so lightly should be deprived of them and the wonder was, holding such opinions as he did, that his fellow Senators even listened to him. Such a miserable politician ought not to be in the Senate. The fact that the women who were asking for the enfranchisement of their sex were amongst the most intelligent citizens in the country was too well known to need proof from her.

Mr. Gaylord had painted a frightful picture of wars between husbands and wives should the latter vote for the opposite camp. "But who would start the war?" queried Amelia. "No man, except one who wished to play the tyrant in his family and enslave his wife's thoughts and actions, would ever utter so silly a reason for not making her an enfranchized citizen." She also considered it a stupid reason for the Senator to argue that suffrage might lead to "bad women" getting into the Legislature and corrupting the law makers. If such women had had a vote long ago, perhaps they would not be bad now, she suggested, and perhaps there would not be so many bad men either. She would sooner trust such women to vote right than many men who then disgraced the ballot. And as to any contamination through queueing with them at the polling booths, women no more feared it than in the streets, public gatherings, in the stores and in various places where they met and brushed by them unmolested. She thought no great harm could come to them through dropping a bit of paper in the same box. "But if there is really danger from such contact with men who make women bad, we can avoid it by having voting places for our own sex away from them."

The Senator's speech had ended with a forecast of what would happen should women ever be permitted to go to the polls. " 'Strife, contention, jealousy, hatred, slander, rivalry, intemperance, licentiousness, temper, retaliation, suicide, suspicion, discord, divorce!'—all these are to come to our good Senator's family when his wife has a right to vote," said Mrs. Bloomer.

"He is doing all he can to avert the dire calamity. But he must remember that not all families are alike, and where he sees only disaster, other men see the dawning of a better day. They do not fear and tremble, but calmly await the time when they can take their wives on their arms, and, side by side, go to the polls and drop in the little paper that declares them equal in rights and privileges."

Then, signing the letter firmly, Amelia gave a murmur of satisfaction. She felt that she had trounced the Senator very effectively and, putting on her bonnet, she went out and delivered the manuscript to the Editor of the *Reporter* in person to make sure that it would be published in the next issue.

That winter she was asked by the literary society to give a talk. She decided to speak on "Housekeeping—Woman's Burden". It had always seemed to her that there was something wrong in the current system of housekeeping. Men had particular branches of business to which they gave their exclusive attention and never attempted to carry on three or four trades at the same time.

Housekeeping comprised at least three trades; those of cook, laundress, and seamstress, to which might be added that of house cleaning. And yet it was expected of women that they should singlehanded successfully carry on these various trades, and at the same time rear children. How long would men undergo a like amount of labour without devising some means of lightening its burdens?

She suggested that as a relief from all this drudgery, a co-operative establishment might be set up in some conveniently central position, fitted out with a number of the latest labour-saving inventions—Mr. Calkin's washing machine and Mr. Isaac Merritt Singer's sewing machine. There might also be a room fitted out as a playroom for tiny children, where one woman could watch over them, whilst their mothers rested at home or went to visit friends for the day. Later, communal cooking facilities might be provided where mothers and children could have their mid-day meals.

Mrs. Bloomer's talk created a great deal of interest. Never before had such ideas been put forward, but perhaps they were a little too advanced for the Council Bluffs of those days. As she had feared, most husbands objected to the project and refused to finance it. If only she had still been Editress of *The Lily*, she might have published an article in it, telling the world at large about her co-operative household chores centre, but unfortunately Mrs. Mary Birdsall had proved an inefficient successor and it had ceased publication.

Amelia would no doubt have gone ahead on her own with her project if a national disaster had not driven all such thoughts from her mind. This was the outbreak of the American Civil War in 1861. As a hater of slavery, she supported the war and was against all compromise.

Her house became the headquarters of all the organizations in Council Bluffs, working for the welfare of the fighting men. She sent a letter to the Convention of Loyal Women in New York City in 1864, regretting that she could not attend as she was so busy despatching warm clothing and hospital stores to those at the front. She and Dexter were fond of children but never had any of their own, and when a friend fell on active service and his widow died of grief, the Bloomers adopted the orphans, a boy and a girl.

In 1865, Amelia's efforts received public acknowledgement when General Grant, commander of the Union armies, asked to meet her and thanked her for setting so fine an example.

It is said that she suggested to the General that a corps of women might be recruited to take over commissariat and clerical work in the army, thus freeing men for more active service. Their uniform might be a short skirt and high laced boots. Needless to say, nothing came of the proposal. Yet again, she was ahead of her time.

When at last victory came to President Lincoln, Mrs. Bloomer was pleased to find that, as a result of what she had done for the soldiers, many in return now supported suffrage for women.

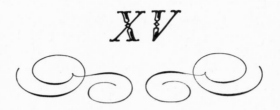

XV

THE WOMEN'S BIBLE

WHEN IN the early part of the nineteenth century, women began to agitate against their lack of civil rights, they were often told by their opponents that their position was divinely ordained, and that any change was contrary to the teachings of the Bible.

It was pointed out to them that woman was made after man, of man, and for man, an inferior being, subject to man. Clergymen told them that their demands were irreligious, dangerous to the stability of the home, the State and the Church. Some ecclesiastics even forbade members of their congregation to take part in the woman's suffrage or the anti-slavery movement, denouncing them as heathen in their tendencies, and liable to undermine the very foundation of society. As the result of this, many women were too timid to risk the displeasure of their pastors and kept aloof from their bolder sisters.

Mrs. Bloomer throughout her life never missed an opportunity for answering back verbally or in print whenever Scripture was quoted by her opponents in support of their arguments. She pointed out that St. Paul in his pronouncements about women had never stated that they were divine commands. Nowhere could she find the words "Thus saith the Lord". What St. Paul had taught only applied to the women of his time, and not to those of the nineteenth century.

Amelia had a very low opinion of Adam. Had he not tried to shield himself by accusing Eve, and putting upon her the punishment of his transgressions? And hadn't all Adams from that time onwards imitated his weakness and meanness by doing the same thing?

Many people had been dissatisfied with the Authorised Version of 1611 and felt that it was time for a more modern translation of the Bible. Eventually, in 1870, the Church of England appointed two companies of scholars to prepare a Revised Version. Negotiations were opened with the Protestant denominations in the United States, and consequently similar companies were formed there.

No woman in either country was invited to serve, which caused great disappointment amongst the feminists. They had hoped that Julia Smith at least might have been approached. She had already translated the whole Bible alone, starting her work many years previously in 1843.

It was the only translation ever made by a woman, and the only one to have been made without assistance from anybody else. She translated the Bible five times—twice from the Hebrew, twice from the Greek, and once from the Latin. Throughout her task, she tried to be as literal as possible.

A number of people considered her wording came closer to the original than earlier translations. It is interesting to note that she used the word "love" instead of "charity" every time.

Miss Smith had undertaken her great work simply out of interest and originally with no idea of publication. In fact, the manuscripts lay in an attic for twenty-five years until she read about the proposed New Version of the Bible, and that it was to be a completely man-controlled undertaking. She then decided that she would try and get her own translation published. But no publishing house was interested, so in 1876 in desperation she took all her savings out of the bank at Hartford where she lived, and paid the local printer to print it.

When the Revised Version of the Bible was at last completed and published, it had an unfavourable reception, and in America Mrs. Elizabeth Cady Stanton took advantage of the opportunity provided by the controversy to launch a project of her own. She formed a committee of eight women under her leadership with the object of publishing commentaries on all passages in the Bible wherever there were any references to women. This was to be done after having first obtained fresh translations of the relevant texts from sympathetic Greek and Hebrew scholars.

It was not until 1895 that these commentaries were published under the title of *The Women's Bible, Part One*. The work had a lengthy preface written by Mrs. Stanton, and most of the comments had her initials after them. These were extremely controversial.

She took the text in the first chapter of Genesis, stating that God created man "in His own image, male and female" as evidence that the Deity was partly feminine, and she suggested that the Trinity really consisted of Father, Mother, and Son.

She contended that in the detailed description of the Creation the least important creatures were mentioned

164

first—creeping things, great sea monsters, every bird of wing, cattle and living things of the earth, the fish of the sea, the birds of the heavens, then man, and last and crowning glory of the whole, woman. If the implications of this description were considered, it could not be maintained that woman was inferior to man. Creation was on an ascending scale. If not, then man was inferior to the creeping things because created after them.

Mrs. Stanton upset some feminists both with her commentaries and with her preface in which she urged those in authority in the Church to ordain women to preach the Gospel and to administer the Sacraments.* She received many letters of disapproval, and in 1896 when the National American Convention of the Suffrage Association of which she was President met in New York, a resolution was proposed by her critics: "That this Association is non-sectarian, being composed of persons of all shades of religious opinion, and has no official connection with the so-called 'Women's Bible'."

There was a long and animated debate. Miss Susan B. Anthony was thoroughly roused, and left the Chair to speak against the resolution.

In an eloquent speech she recalled how Elizabeth Cady Stanton had startled the delegates at the first Women's Rights Convention nearly fifty years previously with her proposal demanding votes for women. It had been said then by some that she had wrecked the movement by making such a revolutionary request. In 1860, when Mrs. Stanton had made a speech before the New York Legislature in favour of a bill making drunkenness grounds for divorce, again the cry had been raised that she would wreck the movement. But it had

* Women's position in the Church has not improved very much since Mrs. Stanton's time; see "Women and Holy Orders" (1967).

gone on from strength to strength, largely thanks to her endeavours. If the present resolution were adopted, it would be a vote of censure upon a woman who was without a peer in intellectual and statesmanlike ability.

Notwithstanding Miss Anthony's speech, the resolution was adopted by fifty-three votes to forty-one.

Although Susan Anthony had defended her life-long friend so ably, she did not really approve of *The Women's Bible*. She felt that their first goal should be obtaining the vote, and that Elizabeth was wasting her time and unnecessarily alienating people who would otherwise have supported them. She told her as much and their relationship became strained in consequence.

Far from being discouraged by all this, Mrs. Stanton worked on with her collaborators and in 1898 a second volume was published with commentaries on Judges, Kings, the Prophets and the Apostles. This volume like the first sold well, and stirred up much comment.

Although many clergymen preached sermons against it, there were a few who found some merit in the work. The Rev. Alexander Kent of Washington, D.C., thought the title unfortunate, but considered the matter contained more commonsense and was more in accordance with Christ's teachings than any other commentary dealing with the same passages. Of all the collaborators of *The Women's Bible*, he found Mrs. Stanton least reverent and tolerant, but he regarded her as the best critic, the most logical, and the most consistent.

Mrs. Bloomer's failing health made her decline an invitation to contribute to this controversial project when it was first mooted. It was published too late for us to know what would have been her reactions to it.

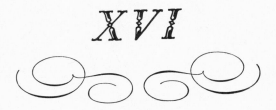

XVI

SHE RESTS IN FAIR VIEW

Althcugh she lived so far from New York, over the years Mrs. Bloomer made several journeys to it. In 1867, she travelled there to attend the first meeting of the Woman Suffrage Association, a new national organization, and was elected one of its Vice-Presidents.

In 1870, owing to her efforts, a Woman Suffrage Society of Iowa came into being and she was elected its first President. Ten years later she was able to write to an old friend in Seneca Falls that all trustees of the Public Library in Council Bluffs were women. "The teachers in the public schools, with one or two exceptions, are women, and a large number of the clerks in the dry goods stores are women."

In the early days many of these young women teachers would live with the Bloomers, and she always strove to give them a pleasant and comfortable home. It irked her that women teachers should not be paid the same salaries as men. She considered that equal amounts of work should receive equal pay and told the

167

school boards so, but despite all her arguments they did nothing about it.

Children, too, were always staying with her. Apart from her adopted son and daughter, nieces and nephews regularly paid her visits—and she made them so happy that they never wanted to leave.

On April 15th, 1890, Amelia and Dexter celebrated the fiftieth anniversary of their wedding. Over a hundred guests crowded their house from three o'clock in the afternoon when the reception began until the evening.

At the front parlour entrance stood Dexter, in a black broad-cloth suit, to greet the visitors. Next to him sat Amelia, still with the same winning smile of welcome that all who met her remembered best. She wore a black satin costume *en train* with a grey damascene front, crêpe lace in the neck, and diamond ornaments. Certainly there was no trace of the dress reformer about her attire on this occasion.

The feelings of feminists towards the couple were best expressed in a letter Miss Anthony sent them. "I hardly believe another twain, made one, where the wife belonged to the school for equal rights for women, have lived more happily, more truly one. Your celebration of your fiftieth wedding day is one of the strongest proofs of the falseness of the charge that equality of political rights for the wife will cause inharmony and disruption of the marriage bond. Hence I rejoice with you, on having reached the golden day of your marriage union, not only for your own sakes, but for our cause's sake as well."

It was a wonderful day for Amelia. She was glad that Dexter, too, was receiving the homage of the towns-people for his work in building up the educational facilities for the young. She was very proud when she heard him called "the father of the public school system of the city".

The last decade of a momentous century had begun. The barriers everywhere against women were beginning to fall. First Wyoming, then Utah, next Colorado gave her the vote. Only three States so far, but Amelia felt that it would not be long before the others followed suit, though she had a presentiment that she herself would not witness the final victory.

She and Dexter had spent a very happy Christmas together with their adopted son and daughter, when on the last day of the year in 1894 she passed away.

She rests in Fair View, high up on a hill above Council Bluffs, which now teems with prosperous people, and among them are women possessing all the rights for which she fought—women dressed in fashions far more advanced than anything she ever wore. One wonders how many of them ever spare her a thought. One hopes that occasionally someone does climb up to Fair View to place, most appropriately, a sheaf of lilies by her modest monument, on which is written very simply: "In Memoriam. Amelia Jenks Bloomer, wife of Dexter C. Bloomer. Aged 76 years, 7 months, and 3 days. A Pioneer in Woman's Enfranchisement."

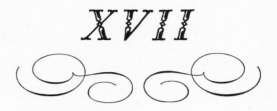

REVIVAL OF THE BLOOMER

IT HAS been truly said that if an outmoded garment is kept long enough, it will one day become fashionable again. By 1860, the Bloomer costume had been forgotten, but in the late eighties it was to be revived in England by Lady Harberton, who founded the National Dress Society, which she later called the Rational Dress Society.

In the spring of 1887, a meeting was held at the Westminster Town Hall to launch the new crusade. Mrs. Oscar Wilde was in the chair and the audience consisted entirely of women. The Viscountess was dressed in Turkish trousers of the finest black satin with a sash round the hips, and a black velvet jacket trimmed with jet *passementerie*, caught together at the waist with a buckle over a full waistcoat of white satin and lace. The costume happened to suit her, although the riding whip, which she cracked to emphasize her points as she spoke, gave her a somewhat mannish appearance.

She began by saying that to cling obstinately to burdensome fetishes of dress was conduct more characteristic of the savage than a civilized Englishwoman. They must therefore hesitate before condemning anything new and ask themselves if their reactions were not motivated by mere prejudice instead of reason. People had long agreed that woman's dress needed reforming, but no real progress had been made to that end.

The clothes of a lady were supposed to show the age and condition of the wearer, whether married or unmarried. The older a woman got, the more unnecessary things it was considered proper for her to pile on her unfortunate person. Her very bonnet became heavier, her mantle and dress of weightier and of richer material, her skirts longer and her improver larger. There was polite laughter at the titled lecturer's quip that age meant having more hair on a lady's head, no matter how it got there. She was certain that the average weight of a grandmother's clothes among the upper classes was not less than fifteen pounds.

Lady Harberton wanted to see women of all ages dressed so that they could take part in muscular games and sport whenever they felt like it. In the present style of dress it was impossible for a woman even to walk properly. If a child of ten years old, in short skirts, walked beside her, the child, though so much shorter, could take longer steps. She mimicked the fatiguing and bad method of walking caused by petticoats, and then illustrated the right mode of walking permitted by her Rational Dress. There was much applause when she held her riding whip level with her head and then kicked it.

Trade opposition to dress reform was a serious obstacle, as most women were the slaves of fashionable dressmakers, who for gain sought to sell as much material as possible, and to make gowns as elaborate as could be. It was all wrong that such people should be allowed to dictate on these matters. Voluminous clothing was exhausting, unhealthy, dirty and dangerous.

"The trouser is not only more comfortable, healthy and clean, but also more decent, as less liable to derangement. The prevailing idea of decency, which exposes the whole of the upper part of a woman's body for the mere sake of display when she is in full dress, but shrouds her legs in layer upon layer of material is a very strange one, and it is time that it was altered. Let us combine to do this, ladies, and prove to the world that union is strength." And bringing down her whip with all her might on some imaginary opponent, her ladyship straddled a chair and sat down to a storm of applause.

The next speaker, Mrs. Pfeiffer, was clad in a very becoming costume, consisting of a Greek chiton of fawn-coloured cashmere, worn over a bodice and divided skirt of terra-cotta silk, belted at the waist and adorned with gold ornaments. She said that they must be careful when designing their Rational Dresses to make them attractive to men, such as the model she was wearing.

A vote of thanks to Lady Harberton was proposed by an authoress, Miss Ada S. Ballin, who had written a book on the subject called *The Science of Dress*. She suggested that Chinese trousers were the most suitable form of attire for both sexes, and that the tight trousers then worn by Englishmen were unhygienic.

Before the meeting concluded, each member in turn mounted the platform so that the other ladies could have the opportunity of studying the individual designs and variations of the Rational Dress. Most of the assembly had followed the example set by their leaders and wore no corsets.

Mrs. Tom Taylor, wife of the leading playwright, was in an elegant creation of pomegranate silk and velvet, the bodice being gathered into a plain yoke. At first sight the audience thought she was wearing a skirt, her trousers were so cunningly cut, until she very obligingly demonstrated that the garment was bifurcated. She was followed on to the platform by her daughter who wore a dark blue serge full blouse with knickerbockers of the same material. Over the latter was draped a plain skirt looped up so as to give the legs full play. She showed the spectators how it could be let down so as to reach the ankles if necessary. There were many murmurs of approval, and several ladies asked for patterns. Both Mrs. and Miss Taylor lived in Lavender Sweep near Clapham Common, and told their listeners how, thanks to their Rational Dresses, they were able to enjoy long walks over its health-giving open acres in all weathers.

The correspondent of the *Pictorial World* who was present, thought the most attractive outfits were those of Mrs. Pfeiffer and a Mrs. Lamond. The latter lady wore a rich black satin evening dress, bordered with a trimming of brown and grey ribbon. It was made on the Greek chiton principle, but with a train. "The effect was most elegant and if all Rational Dresses resembled these two, there would be no difficulty in reconciling fastidious man to their use."

As the audience dispersed, handbills in which the Society's objects were listed were distributed to those not already members. These were "to protest against the introduction of any fashion in dress that either deforms the figure, impedes the movements of the body, or in any way tends to injure the health".

It further protested against "the wearing of tightly-fitting corsets, of high-heeled or narrow-toed boots and shoes; of heavily-weighted skirts, as rendering healthy exercise almost impossible; and of all tie-down cloaks or other garments impeding the movements of the arms. It protests against crinolines or crinolettes of any kind as ugly and deforming. The maximum weight of clothing (without shoes) approved of by the Rational Dress Society does not exceed seven lbs."

In April, 1888, the Society started publishing a quarterly *Gazette*. The first issue contained advice on the most discussed item of clothing they sponsored—the "Divided Skirt".

The Editress informed her readers that there were two variations of this garment, both equally liked. "That known as the 'Harberton' is narrow—about half a yard wide at the ankle—and has a narrow box pleat round it. This is usually not continued on the inner side, so as to avoid fullness between the ankles.

"The 'Wilson' is quite different. It is about a yard and a half wide round each leg. The pleats are carried up nearly to the waist, but so arranged as to fall outside the legs. Owing to the quantity of stuff required to make it, only very light materials should be used. Patterns can be obtained at the Depot."

The Editress added that she had received encouraging news that "the 'Divided Skirt' had even come to be considered as a possibility for tricycling and other active exercise". It is interesting to note that the late Queen Mary in her youth spent many a rainy afternoon tricycling round the ballroom at Sandringham.

The first number of the *Gazette* also described a "Rational System of Underclothing" which included "the Rational Dress Society's chemise (sometimes called the 'Survival') of which patterns can be obtained on application at the Society's Depot".

This Depot was housed at 11 Sloane Street, and conducted on the ready money system. "Consequently we
are able to offer our customers goods at low prices.
Underclothing, rational corsets and bodices, and divided
skirts are among the articles that we provide."

Later that year, the *Gazette* proudly told its readers
that at the Paris Exhibition "an original pattern of the
'Divided Skirt' is one of the most curious exhibits in the
British Section on the *Champs de Mars*. It attracts the
attention of the *Parisiennes* to an amazing extent and is
the subject of much voluble comment and discussion
not unaccompanied by admiration. This wonderful
article is exhibited in the case of Mr. John Manby of
the *Rue Aube*."

About this time, a sensation was caused in Paris, too,
when the well known traveller, Mme. Dieulafoy, was
turned out of a theatre by a Commissioner of Police
because she went there with cropped hair, wearing a
Persian style Bloomer costume.

Meanwhile, the Rational Dress Society prospered and
increased its membership, thanks to the lectures given
by Viscountess Harberton, Mrs. Oscar Wilde, and Mrs.
Carmichael Stopes (mother of Dr. Marie Stopes). One
of the latter's most successful talks was published in
Oscar Wilde's *Woman's World*, thanks to his wife's
persuasion.

Rational Dress received a boost in the nineties, when
the safety bicycle, with pneumatic tyres, enabled women
to take up the sport. Conservative ladies such as Princess Maud had their skirts weighted with shot when
they went a-pedalling. Those in the middle camp ventured forth in "artistically cut skirts, artfully arranged
to hang in even portions each side of the saddle" as a
fashion writer of the period puts it—in other words

Divided Skirts which were divided in action, but looked united at rest. The most popular version of the Divided Skirt became known as the *"Pédaleuse"*.

The advanced young woman dashed up hill and down dale in loud checked knickerbockers, gaiters, Norfolk jacket and Robin Hood hat. Mrs. Bloomer, then in her seventies, had read about this with approval, and had been amused to learn that this new form of the costume she had launched over forty years previously had been given the name of Bloomers.

Amelia's old colleague, Elizabeth Cady Stanton, was delighted when she heard about it. *The Wheelman* which catered for devotees of this latest craze commissioned an article from her, wherein she was asked to deal with such questions as to whether women should cycle, what they should wear, and whether they should ride on Sundays.

"If women can ride, God intended they should do so," she wrote. "They should wear what they find most convenient and comfortable. I believe that if a woman prefers a run in the open air on Sunday to a prosy sermon in a close church, she should ride by all means."

And for other kinds of sport such as lawn tennis and sea bathing, the old Bloomer costume with modifications became the vogue.

Then three-quarters of a century later, in 1967, a new Bloomer Look appeared. Ironically enough, it was the capital of fashion, deriders of the 1851 Costume, that produced this shrunken modern version of it.

On Monday, January 23rd, the *couturiers* began displaying their new collections to the world. In the *Evening News* that night, Miss Ann Beveridge told readers that in the spring, if Paris had its way, Bloomers would "peep boldly beneath the hemlines of short as ever smocks and shifts".

Louis Féraud, the go-ahead young designer, had been the first to reveal his secrets—beguiling bloomers in acid colours, aimed at the young and gay, and to be worn with slit hip mini-dresses, and coat dresses.

In the *Daily Mail* of January 30th, Judy Innes reported that the fashion writers watching the usually conservative *couturier* Ungaro's show could hardly believe their eyes when the evening outfits appeared. "Even Ungaro has been seduced by the current craze for Bloomers. His Bloomers, in fact, bloomed more ebulliently than anyone else's, full and short and jewel-edged, under short, full smock tops with jewelled yokes."

The *Daily Mail* next day also gave the news that Fenwicks of Bond Street had won the race to be the first West End store to offer Bloomers to its customers. From that morning, they would be making available to personal shoppers, and to shy ones through the post, chic Bloomers in white *broderie anglaise* and trimmed with pastel bows. They would be found in the department selling at-home outfits for lounging, though Fenwicks were careful to point out that this novelty could be worn equally well as an under-garment, in bed or to a party.

"British manufacturers know a trend when they see one," ran the article. Our designers were rushing their Bloomer Suits into production. "Some are simply adding matching Bloomers to ready designed mini-dresses. Others are bringing out special lines."

Some even asserted that London had thought of the Bloomer Look before Paris, as a month prior to the French showing their models, an English manufacturer had brought out "Bloomers for Bridesmaids".

In the *Evening News* for January 3rd, under the

caption of "Heres Comes The Bridesmaid", appeared a photograph of the lower part of a young lady wearing, instead of a skirt, knickers trimmed with two overlapping ruffs above the knees. "This, it is claimed, is what the well-dressed bridal attendant will be wearing this year," went the news paragraph. "The outfit, a frilly pyjama style in pink chiffon with matching layered ruffs, was shown in London today in a new range of hire-wear."

By February 17th, Miss Beveridge was able to write in her paper: "Fashion—strange as it may seem—has gone head over heels on Bloomers. Already, London shops report a mounting Bloomer boom. First-off-the-mark shoppers are snatching them off the rails, and buyers are saying they are confident of a 'sensational success'." But she wondered whether one would really see "those baggy Bloomers and frilly knickers pounding across the platform to catch the early morning train".

The Bloomer Suits she had seen were all-purpose garments that could be worn for play, the beach or bed. They were all in one, like mini cat-suits with blouson frilly legs, and should be worn with bare feet or sandals.

As for Bloomer dresses, most manufacturers were making them wide-legged in organdie, or in a frilly knicker style to peep coyly under the hem of a mini-tent or tunic. With these dresses, matching tights, now down in price, were a MUST!

In an amusing article in the *Evening News* of February 2nd, Patricia Johnson described how she went to a party one evening in Bloomers, complete with navy over-tunic, and with her hair arranged in Mary Pickford ringlets.

"I walked in and the men turned away to smile. Disaster, I felt, was imminent. My first comment was from a girl in a minus mini-skirt. 'Oh,' she said, 'those

178

Bloomers look super. I'm furious!' The party began to throng up, and I found myself in the middle of a cluster of men who couldn't take their eyes off my Bloomers.

" 'They're far sexier than mini-skirts,' said one man, 'because they leave something to the imagination.' Another raised his champagne glass and said, 'Mini-skirts are dead. Long live Bloomers!' "

Bicycling fashions, too, in 1967, completed a full turn of the fashion wheel, according to Miss Penny Graham of the *Daily Express* in which she wrote on April 14th that "bloomers, named after that intrepid feminist, Amelia Bloomer, who started the vogue for them in the 1850s, and the old style knicker-bockers are back in the wheel world".

A picture accompanying the article showed an attractive young blonde on her bicycle in a modern Bloomer two piece. "This is made in turquoise and white checked cotton, and the *broderie anglaise* frill round the pants just peep under the dress when you are standing. Eminently suitable for bicycling and parties."

It certainly would be a dull world without women's changing fashions. It is interesting to reflect that the modern girl wears less in the street than Amelia Bloomer wore in bed. What will tomorrow bring? Let that expert on fashion, James Laver, have the last word. In one of the lyrics he has written for a new musical play, he asks:

> "What will they be wearing next?
> I own I'm exceedingly vexed
> To think that the history of clothes
> Should come, at the end of the road,
> To a couple of plumes in the hair,
> A bangle, a necklace and—woad!
> What will they be wearing next?

What will they be wearing next?
I own I am much perplexed.
Will it be hobble skirts
Or big balloon sleeves,
Will they go back to Eden
And just put on leaves?
What will they be wearing next?. . ."

APPENDIX

A S WOMEN'S wear becomes scantier, more cases arise of daring dressers failing to crash the fashion barrier at some hotel or restaurant. The first woman to challenge such discrimination in the courts was the Irish-born Viscountess Harberton. Apart from her Rational Dress Society, she also founded the Short Dress League, members of which undertook to have their walking dresses not less than five inches off the ground and to let knickerbockers and gaiters take the place of ordinary petticoats.

On April 5th, 1899, at the Surrey Quarter Sessions, held at Kingston-on-Thames, Martha Jane Sprague, wife of Sidney Sprague, was indicted for that she, being the keeper of a common inn for the reception and accommodation of travellers, called the Hautboy Hotel at Ockham in the county of Surrey, did, on October 27th, 1898, without sufficient cause and not regarding her duty as an innkeeper, wilfully and unlawfully neglect and refuse to supply Florence Wallace Harberton, wife of Viscount Harberton, then being a traveller, with victuals, which she then required, and for which she was willing to pay. The defendants pleaded: "Not guilty."

Lord Coleridge, Q.C., in opening the case, said that the prosecution was of an unusual character, and was undertaken by the Cyclists' Touring Club against Mrs. Sprague for refusing to supply Lady Harberton with luncheon by reason of the latter appearing at the hotel in what was called "rational" cycling costume. The case was brought to test the general principle.

The law had been laid down by *Coleridge, J.* in *Rex v. Ivens*, 7 C. & P. 213, at p. 219: "An indictment lies against an innkeeper who refuses to receive a guest, he having at the time room in his house, and either the price of the guest's entertainment being tendered to him or such circumstances occurring as will dispense with that tender. This law is founded on good sense. The innkeeper is not to select his guests. He has no right to say to one, you shall come into my inn, and to another, you shall not, as everyone coming and conducting himself in a proper manner has a right to be received." And later on: "If a person came to an inn drunk, or behaved in an indecent or improper manner, I am of opinion that the innkeeper is not to receive him."

That being the law, the question was whether Lady Harberton in applying for admittance in rational costume, was guilty of indecent or improper conduct. He (the learned counsel) would show the jury a photograph of Lady Harberton taken in the dress she wore upon the occasion in question, from which it appeared that she was clothed from the crown of her head to the soles of her feet. If the jury thought that she was properly clothed, though they might not like the cut of her garments, then Mrs. Sprague had no right to refuse her admittance to the hotel. If the jury decided that Mrs. Sprague was justified in refusing admittance to Lady Harberton on account of her clothes, then on some future day, when everyone admired rational costume, the jury might be held up as purblind and perverted.

Lady Harberton, examined, said that she was a member of the Cyclists' Touring Club and invariably wore national costume when cycling. On October 27th, 1898, she left home for a bicycle ride. She agreed that the photograph she was shown was a photograph of her in the dress she wore that day. She rode to Ockham and went to the Hautboy Hotel and said that she wanted some lunch. Mrs. Sprague said: "No, not in that dress. I do not admit people in that dress." Witness said that she had come from London and was hungry and tired and must have luncheon. Mrs. Sprague replied: "You can have it in a private room if you pay for it." Witness answered that she did not care what room she had it in, but she expected to be served as a member of the Cyclists' Touring Club on the usual terms, and she showed the landlady her badge.

Mrs. Sprague said that in that case she must go to a room on the other side of the bar, and after making her leave her bicycle in the stable led her into the room in question, which was occupied by four men, two smoking and two in working dress. Witness described the smell of the room as abominable. She refused to stay in that room. Mrs. Sprague insisted it was all she could offer her. Witness then rode off to Cobham and got lunch there.

When cross-examined by Mr. Horace Avory for the defence, Lady Harberton revealed that she had walked up Regent Street in rational dress, but admitted that she wore evening dress to the theatre.

Evidence was given by Ernest Richard Shipton, secretary of the Cyclists' Touring Club, who stated that Lady Harberton had complained to the Club immediately after the incident. In cross-examination he agreed that the prosecution had occasioned a considerable divergence of opinion among the members of his Club, but the large majority approved of it. A passage from the Club's handbook was read to witness in which the advice was given to ladies to carry a skirt so as to cover the "rationals" when off the machine. This was merely the opinion of the writer of "Hints on Touring" in the handbook, and was in no sense the official opinion of the Club.

Avory for the defence submitted there was no case to go to the jury. There was no evidence of a refusal to supply victuals. At the most, there was only a refusal to supply it in a particular room. There was admittedly an offer to supply refreshment in the bar parlour. No person had a right to choose any particular room.

The Chairman asked: "Suppose the landlord said he would only supply victuals in the coal cellar?"

Avory replied that was an extreme case. But was an indictment to lie against the landlord because a fastidious lady disliked the smell of smoke? It would be a most dangerous thing to leave such a case to the jury. It was a question of taste. There were many ladies who liked the smell of smoke.

After the Chairman had ruled that the case must go to the jury, Avory addressed them. He claimed that it was an abuse of the criminal law to indict Mrs. Sprague in a case such as this. That law had been laid down when people travelled by coach, when they were dependent for their food and beds upon the inns, and when the roads were unsafe to travel on at night. If the judges who had laid down that law could see to what use it was being turned, they would turn in their graves. This prosecution was nothing but an advertisement of the Cyclists' Touring Club and of rational dress for ladies. Mrs. Sprague was not acting in a spirit of prudery, but in the interest of good order in her hotel. Everyone knew that there might be men in a coffee room in an hotel on the Portsmouth Road who might make jokes about ladies coming into the room in rational dress, and so create a disturbance. The jury had not to say whether ladies ought to wear this style of dress when cycling. They had only to say whether Lady Harberton was refused food.

When examined by Mr. Avory, Mrs. Sprague declared she was sure Lady Harberton was without reproach, but it would be fatal to her business to admit to the coffee room certain people who had frequented the Portsmouth Road. She had seen ladies in skin tights. Therefore she made it a general rule not to admit ladies in rational dress.

The Chairman in summing up said that an innkeeper could not refuse to supply a traveller with food and lodging without some lawful excuse. The question whether ladies should or not wear rational dress was not in dispute. An innkeeper could not refuse to supply food because of the particular shape of the dress of the traveller. The only question, therefore, was whether there was a refusal to supply food in a decent and proper room. Nor, in his opinion, was a guest entitled to have a room exactly to his or her taste. The jury must judge by the requirements of ordinary and reasonable persons.

The jury retired to consider their verdict, and, after a short deliberation, they returned one of "Not Guilty".

Few members of Lady Harberton's Short Dress League were willing to fight for their cause as resolutely as she did. *Cycling* for April 23rd, 1898, states: "The question of rational dress depends apparently on when it is worn. At a gymnastic display in Dublin recently by an English ladies' team, the costume adopted during the exercise consisted of jersey and knickers, with short skirts to the knees. When these ladies turned out for the musical cycle-ride, however, they had changed the above-mentioned garb for ordinary skirts evidently fearing the effects of rational dress upon the feelings of the spectators."

185

SELECTED BIBLIOGRAPHY

BALLIN, Ada. *The Science of Dress*. (London, 1893).

Bentley's Miscellany. Volume 30. (London, 1851)

BIRNEY, Catherine. *Sarah and Angelina Grimké*. (Boston, 1885)

BLACKWELL, Alice Stone. *Lucy Stone*. (Boston, 1920)

BLOOMER, Dexter C. *Amelia Bloomer*. (Boston, 1895)

BODICHON, Barbara. *Women and Work*. (New York, 1859)

CALHOUN, Arthur. *A Social History of the American Family*. (Cleveland, 1917–19)

CELNART, Mme. *Book of Politeness*. (Philadelphia, 1847)

CLARKE, H. G. *The English Maiden, Her Moral and Domestic Duties*. (London, 1848)

CROMWELL, Otelia. *Lucretia Mott*. (Harvard University, 1958)

CUNNINGTON, C. Willet. *Feminine Attitudes in the Nineteenth Century*. (London, 1936)

CUNYNGHAME, Sir A. A. T. *A Glimpse at the Great Western Republic*. (London, 1851)

DAVIS, Paulina Wright. *A History of the National Women's Rights Movement for Twenty Years*. (New York, 1871)

DORR, Rheta. *Susan B. Anthony*. (New York, 1928)

EARLE, Alice. *Two Centuries of Costume in America*. (New York, 1903)

Englishwoman's Year Book, The. (London, 1884-5-6-7-8-9)

ERSKINE, F. J. *Lady Cycling*. (London, 1897)

FLEXNER, Eleanor. *Century of Struggle*. (Harvard University, 1959)

FOWLER, O. S. *Intemperance and Tight Lacing*. (London, 1898)

186

GARRISON, Wm. Lloyd. *The Story of His Life Told By His Children*. (4 vols., New York, 1885–9)

Godey's Lady's Book & Ladies' American Magazine. (Volumes for 1851–3)

GREEN, H. & M. *The Pioneer Mothers of America*. (New York, 1912)

GRIMKE, Sarah. *Letter on the Equality of the Sexes*. (Boston, 1838)

HARPER, Ida. *The Life & Work of Susan B. Anthony*. (Indianapolis, 1898)

HAYS, Elinor. *Morning Star, a Biography of Lucy Stone*. (New York, 1961)

Ladies' Journal, The. (London, volumes for 1851–2.)

Lily, The. (Seneca Falls, 1849–53, Mount Vernon, 1853–55, Richmond, Indiana, 1855–8)

Illustrated London Almanack, The. (Volumes for 1850–52.)

Illustrated London News, The. (Volumes for 1850–52.)

LUTZ, Alma. *Susan B. Anthony*. (Boston, 1959)
    Created Equal—Biography of E. C. Stanton. (New York, 1940)

MCCRACKEN, Elizabeth. *The Women of America*. (New York, 1904)

MORRIS, Richard. *Studies in the History of American Law*. (New York, 1958)

MOTT, James & Lucretia. *Letters, edited by Anna Hallowell*. (Boston 1884)

Playgoer & Literary Tatler, The. Numbers 1 to 18. (London, 1851)

Proceedings of the General Anti-Slavery Convention. (London, 1840)

Punch. (London, 1850 to 1898)

Rational Dress Society's Gazette, The. Numbers 1 to 6. (London, 1888–9)

RIEGEL, R. *American Feminists*. (University of Kansas, 1963)

SALMON, Lucy. *Domestic Service*. (New York, 1897)

SANFORD, Miss. *Woman in Her Social & Domestic Character*. (Boston, 1844)

SMITH, Albert, & LEECH, John. *The Month, a view of passing subjects and manners*. (London, 1851)

SPRAGUE, Wm. *Women and the West*. (Boston, 1940)

STANTON, Elizabeth Cady, in collaboration with Susan B. Anthony & Matilda Gage. *History of Woman Suffrage*. Volumes I & II. (New York, 1881)

STANTON, E. C. *Eighty Years & More—Reminiscences*. (New York, 1898)

STANTON, Theodore, & BLATCH, Harriot. *Elizabeth Cady Stanton*. (New York, 1922)

Theatrical Journal, The. (London, 1851)

Times, The. (London, 1851)

Woman's World. (London, 1887–95)

WOOLSON, Abba. *Woman in American Society*. (Boston, 1873)

INDEX

Albert, Prince, 15, 23, 24
Anneké, Mathilde Franceska, 98, 108, 109
Anthony, Daniel, 115 ff.
Anthony, Susan Brownell, 64, 83, 86, 87, 111, 115 ff., 126, 151, 152, 168
Anti-Slavery Convention in New York, 99
Anti-Slavery Society, 96
Aylesbury, Lady, 52

Ballin, Miss Ada S., 172
Bennett, James Gordon, 97, 98, 102
Bentley's Miscellany, 73
Beveridge, Ann, 176, 178
Birdsall, Mrs. Mary, 136, 161
Blackwell, Elizabeth, 29, 100
Blackwell, Henry, 100
Blackwell, Samuel, 100
Blockley, J. J., 75
Bloomer, Amelia Jenks, 12 ff., 19, 36, 40 ff., 44 ff., 52 ff., 56 ff., 61, 62, 64, 65, 73, 74, 82 ff., 91 ff., 100 ff., 104, 112 ff., 127, 128, 132 ff., 137 ff., 146, 148 ff., 157 ff., 162, 163, 166 ff., 179; birth, 15; marriage, 16; writes for *The Water Bucket*, 17, 18; attends First Women's Rights Convention, 33; starts up *The Lily*, 37 ff.; becomes Deputy Postmaster, 39; her picture in the Bloomer Costume appears in the *Illustrated London News*, 66; attends Whole World's Temperance

Bloomer, Amelia Jenks—*cont.*
Convention, 98; attacked by James Gordon Bennett, 102; proposes appeal to women of Europe, 106; elected a Vice-President of Women's Rights Convention, 110; introduces Miss Anthony to Mrs. Stanton, 117, 126; departure from Seneca Falls, 129, 130; becomes Assistant Editor of *Western Home Visitor*, 130, 131; parts with *The Lily*, 136; impressive speech to Nebraska House of Representatives, 145; gives up wearing the Bloomer Costume, 147; work during Civil War, 161; death, 169
Bloomer, Dexter C., 15 ff., 33, 36, 39, 52, 95, 96, 128 ff., 132, 133, 135 ff., 150, 168, 169
Bloomer Institute, Lowell, 62
Bloomer, London Committee, 68
Bloomerism in Arbroath, 80
Bloomerism in California, 62
Bloomerism at the Crystal Palace, 67
Bloomerism in Edinburgh, 79
Bloomerism in Piccadilly, 66
Bloomers, Association of, 66
Bowring, Dr., 25
British & Foreign Anti-Slavery Society, 24
Brown, Rev. Antoinette, 97 ff.
Bryant, Wm. Cullen, 97
Buckingham, Mrs. L. S., 73

191

DATE DUE

MAY 1 1981			
APR 2 1982			
MAR 18 1983			
NOV 23 '90			
APR 26 '91			

DEMCO 38-297